Pensamiento Universitario
Iberoamericano

THOMAS PIKETTY
IS WRONG

by

CARLOS OBREGÓN

THOMAS PIKETTY IS WRONG

1st English edition, 2015, Pensamiento Universitario Iberoamericano
Reserved Rights® 2015, Carlos Federico Obregón Díaz

Design: Ricardo Pascoe (Spot-ON)www.spot0n.com

I wish to express my gratitude to Carlo Benetti, Álvaro de Garay, Jorge Mariscal and Ricardo Solís for their valuable comments in an earlier version of this manuscript. I am particularly grateful to Jorge A. Preciado for many fruitful discussions and for critical reading and careful typesetting of this manuscript.

Contents

List of Tables

Preamble

What is under discussion is the dynamics of capitalism as a whole. If Piketty is right, there will be long-term economic laws that will necessarily generate class conflict: the confrontation between the richest 10% with the rest of the society. Moreover, if his convergence mechanism were right, this would mean that both poverty and the highly unequal global income distribution between countries would soon become events of the past.

In this essay we argue that Piketty is wrong—no such long-term economic laws exist. Moreover, we will cast serious doubts on the likelihood of his convergence mechanism.

Capitalism is not about wealth, but about capital. One cannot build a theory of capitalism based only on wealth distributional effects since these are intimately related to the production side of the economy. We argue that Piketty has confused wealth with capital and, in doing so, he has undermined the dynamic role of the markets. Economic agents optimize and neither the rate of return of capital nor the net savings rate can be relatively rigid as Piketty assumes.

As Piketty states, long-term global growth is mainly explained by the accumulation and diffusion of knowledge; but growth is also associated to capital—capital is productive. The productivity of capital is related to the elasticity of substitution between capital and labor, and we will show that Piketty's economic dynamics is incompatible with the empirical estimates of such elasticity. Moreover, saving is done to stimulate growth; therefore, there has to be a positive relation between the savings rate and the growth rate of the economy; a relation that, as we will show, Piketty undermines.

Economic growth is not only intertwined to knowledge and the productivity of capital but it is also interconnected with the size of the market. As Adam Smith argued, a large market fosters technological development. In developed capitalism the enlargement of the market size is enmeshed with the economic participation of the middle class. Therefore, Piketty's capitalism dynamics is wrong. He undermines two crucial factors that characterize global capitalism: the rapid growth of the middle class in developed countries and the lasting highly unequal distribution between poor and rich countries. One of the key problems of the developing economies is precisely that they do not have the required middle class size.

The discussion of whether Piketty is right or wrong is very important. If he is right the policy focus will have to be in reducing class conflict: a tax policy for capital would be the solution to the global economy, which by itself would take care of the problem of growth, particularly of unequal countries growth. If, as we will show, he is wrong, then the economy itself will not solve the problem of growth; we will need special policies to promote development in the poor countries and the focus would have to be in eliminating poverty and fostering the right institutional policies for housing, urban development, education and so on.

Abstract

Piketty (2014) argues that there are long-run fundamental laws in capitalism that will necessarily concentrate the income in favor of the privileged 1 or 10% of the population. Piketty's two fundamental laws are really theoretical propositions which presume relative rigidity in the rate of return of capital, r, and in the net savings rate, s_n. Such propositions, we will show, are incompatible with both: 1) the seventy-five years of studies estimating the value of the elasticity of substitution between capital and labor, and 2) the theoretical models of savings optimizing behaviour. In this essay we will argue that Piketty's laws are wrong, and that they contradict the essence itself of market dynamics. Economic agents optimize and neither r nor s_n can remain relatively stable as Piketty supposes.

Using empirical estimates of the long-run elasticity of substitution between capital and labor, and analyzing the relationship between the net savings rate, s_n, and the real growth rate of the economy, g, we will show that Piketty (2014)'s forecast for the second half of the twenty-first century is inadequate. We propose alternative forecasts.

The introduction presents a brief summary of Piketty's general dynamics of capitalist societies; the first section analyzes the dynamics of the rate of return of capital, r; the second section reviews the dynamics of the savings rate, s; the third section discusses the forecast for g, the real rate of growth of the economy; the fourth section shows alternative scenarios and concludes. Finally, the epilogue provides general comments related to income distribution, the rise of the middle class and underdevelopment.

Findings summary

Piketty's dynamics of capitalism is incompatible with seventy-five years of literature estimating the elasticity of substitution between capital and labor, σ. Piketty has argued that this is likely due to the fact that such elasticity will likely increase in the long run. Recently, however, Chirinko and Mallick (2014), and, Karabarbounis and Neiman (2014), have estimated which are the potential long-run effects on the gross elasticity, σ^{gross}. Their estimates give a range for σ^{gross} between 0.857 and 1.25, a range that is still incompatible with Piketty.

Piketty and Zucman (2014) argue that a net elasticity, σ^{net}, between 1.2 and 1.6 explains the mutual increase of α, the capital income share, and β, the capital/income ratio, from 1970 to 2010 in the developed countries—and Piketty (2014) moves that to 1.3 to 1.6. But, as Rognlie (2014) has shown, σ^{net} is substantially lower than σ^{gross}, and therefore Piketty's net elasticity of 1.2 to 1.6 corresponds to a gross elasticity of 1.93 to 2.56, which is out of range of any empirical estimate. Using the long-run range for σ^{gross} of 0.857 and 1.25, the elasticity between α and β, is negative and not positive as Piketty has argued. Looking at the historical data of the main developed countries, from 1970 to 2010, when α goes up β also goes up as Piketty argues, but non-housing β at book value, β_{nhbv}, goes down. This implies that the positive relationship between α and β that Piketty finds empirically is only due to speculative waves and price effects that cannot be the base of a long-run forecast. Specifically it is due to two factors: 1) A speculative housing wave that increased not only the prices but also lead to over-construction, and 2) the fact that the main stock markets have been going up since 1970, causing β at market value, β_{mv}, to get closer to its book value, β_{bv}. Therefore, β_{mv} increases even though β_{bv} is decreasing, only due to the fact that β_{mv} gets closer to β_{bv}.

What does it mean that β_{mv} is closer to β_{bv}? For most countries, at the macro level, β_{mv} is less than β_{bv}, meaning that stock holders discount the market price in relationship to the book value, likely due to the uncertainty over the adequate management of the assets in the books; Piketty has argued that this reflects stock owners' lack of control on assets usage. Hence, when the market value gets closer to the book value it means that share holders are more confident about the management of the assets and, therefore, discount the market price of the stock less in relationship to its book value. But this price effect has nothing to do with productivity.

Piketty (2014)'s forecast for the second half of the twenty-first century implies a growth rate of the economy of $g = 1.5\%$, and a net savings rate of 10%. Consequently, we have a private wealth β of 667%. Moreover, he assumes that the rate of return of capital, r, remains in 4.3%, the same value it had in 1990–2010, and then α becomes 28.7%. Notice that, if r remains constant, when β increases from 440% in 2010 to 667% in 2100, this implies an infinite σ, a fully robotized economy. Then, Piketty (2014)'s forecast does not relate to the characteristics of the production function in a productive capitalist economy—it does not relate to capital. It is based upon short to medium term wealth sequels due to speculative waves and price effects.

Using Piketty's forecasted $\beta = 667\%$ and σ^{gross} in the range of 0.857 to 1.25, we get an exaggerate downfall in α, in the wide range of 14.85% to 45.29% in relationship to the initial reference α. We also have a very low r, compared to historical statistics, in the range of 1.55% to 2.42%. Obviously something is wrong, either β or the range of σ^{gross}. Piketty argues that the historical data shows that the elasticity must be higher, but this argument is wrong since the historical positive co-movement between α and β is only due to the speculative housing wave and to the fact that β_{mv} is getting closer to β_{bv}. In the very long run the relationship between β_{mv} and β_{bv} must be stable and the speculative housing wave must recede. Therefore, what must be wrong in the forecast has to be β. Since β is equal to the net savings rate divided by the real growth rate of the economy, $\beta = s_n/g$, then either s_n or g are incorrectly forecasted. If we assume that g is correctly forecasted, then s_n must be off range.

Krusell and Smith (2015) showed, in models where the economic agents optimize, that both the gross and the net savings rates are functions of g. They also showed that these models explain well the American economy. But, given the available data for the world economy it is not possible to calibrate these models. However, in a Solow model, with a given gross savings rate, the net savings rate becomes a function of g. Hence, using empirical evidence of the main developed countries for the gross savings rate during 1991–2010, which fell in relation to previous periods due to the fall of g, we have estimated the net savings rate corresponding to a growth rate of the economy of 1.5% assumed by Piketty for the second half of the twenty-first century. We have obtained a weighted average of $s_n = 6.40\%$, substantially lower than Piketty's 10%. Since Piketty's overall assumption that g globally converges to that of the developed economies, this is a good estimate corresponding to a growth rate of 1.5%. With $s_n = 6.40\%$ we have that $\beta = 427\%$ and using σ^{gross} in the range of 0.857 to 1.25, we obtain an r in the range of 4.47% to 4.55%, which is compatible with the historical evidence and with Piketty's intuition that r should be around 4%. Since initially β was 440%, $\beta = 427\%$ represents a small downfall and produces modest increasing returns, therefore α actually increases. It must be noted that α increases when β falls and not when β goes up as Piketty has proposed. Moreover, α increases very modestly, in the range of 0.8% to 2.6% in relationship to its initial value. This implies that the capitalists will increase their income share between 0.16% and 0.5%; quite different from Piketty's forecast which implied an increase of 9.75%.

We also estimate an alternative scenario with g growing at 2.1% instead of Piketty's 1.5%. In this case $s_n = 8.07\%$, and $\beta = 384\%$. The higher fall in β then triggers more significant increasing returns and the estimated r goes up to the range of 5.1% to 5.47%. Consequently α increases more aggressively but still in a moderate range of 3.65% to 11.10% above its initial reference value. This would imply that the capitalists' income share would increase between 0.69% and 2.1%, again much lower than Piketty's forecasted 9.75%.

We conclude that there is not an invisible hand that will necessarily drive capitalism towards income concentration in favor of the capitalists. Markets work and it is difficult to envision that, only due to economic forces, the income distribution will worsen significantly; and in any case, if this happened, it would be due to capital scarcity and not due to capital abundance as Piketty has suggested.

Introduction: Piketty's capitalist society general dynamics

Piketty argues that the world economy will reduce its growth rate in the twenty-first century and that there are fundamental laws of capital accumulation that will necessarily lead to a substantial increase in the capital/income ratio, β, as well as in the capital's share of income, α; and because wealth is heavily concentrated, this will imply a considerable worsening of the personal income distribution, particularly in favor of the richest 1% or 10%. The consequence, is that the inheritance flow will increase, and a greater proportion of income will be derived from rents on inherited wealth and less from income related to one's own effort. Therefore, the process of capital accumulation threatens the core values of meritocratic societies. The natural consequences of the general laws of capital accumulation had been in the past ameliorated by exogenous shocks—such as the two wars and the policies adopted as a consequence—but the tendency will be reestablished in the twenty-first century. Therefore, argues this author, it is needed that institutions adopt policies opposing such general tendency of capitalism, so he proposes a global tax on capital.

Piketty distinguishes forces pushing toward convergence and divergence. The principal convergence mechanism, particularly related to the income distribution between countries, is the diffusion of knowledge and the investment in training and skills. The main divergence mechanism is the process of capital accumulation itself. The divergence forces are of such magnitude that, if they are not opposed by adequate institutional policies, they will destroy the meritocratic society. There are also other proposals from Piketty such as the argument that the salaries of top american executives are better explained by power relationships and not by marginal productivity. Through all his book there are interesting comments and discussions about several topics in economics. Some of them are of great relevance, like the need and convenience to regulate and tax capital invested in fiscal paradises.

Piketty's first conclusion is that "The history of the distribution of wealth has always been deeply political, and it cannot be reduced to purely economic mechanisms". His second conclusion is that "... the dynamics of wealth distribution reveal powerful mechanisms pushing alternatively toward convergence and divergence", Piketty (2014, p. 21). And "The crucial fact is that no matter how potent a force, the diffusion of knowledge and skills may be, especially in promoting convergence between countries, it can nevertheless be thwarted and overwhelmed by powerful forces pushing in the opposite direction, toward greater inequality", Piketty (2014, p. 22). In summary, the divergence force of capital accumulation is more powerful than the convergence force of diffusion of knowledge, but it can be opposed politically by institutional policies; therefore what is needed is a political decision and Piketty proposes the global income tax—and understanding the complications of such tax he suggests to start with the European Union.

This author uses both empirical and theoretical instruments. His empirical analysis centres in developed countries but his general dynamics, he argues, is also applicable to under-developed countries and to the global mechanics of capitalism. Empirically, he constructs an impressive database of income and wealth in the main developed countries. Theoretically, he uses a neoclassical model of economic growth with peculiar characteristics that he introduces. Piketty reopens the question of the income distribution in capitalism. If anything, it becomes clearly established that the capitalist system does not necessarily solve the income distribution problem. The income distribution depends crucially in the institutional arrangement on which the capitalist structure exists. Piketty's three critical contributions are: 1) he reopens the discussion on the topic of income distribution, 2) the creation of a relevant database which, despite requiring improvements, allows such discussion, and 3) his insistence that the income distribution amongst the factors of production is not necessarily stable.

But this author further pretends to unravel the fundamental dynamics of capitalism. His book then inserts itself in the long tradition of classical economics, particularly the one of Ricardo and Marx. For Piketty, the dynamics of capitalism is given by what he calls the two fundamental laws of capitalism, which necessarily imply a social conflict amongst social classes, particularly between the richest 1% or 10% and the rest of society.

Chapter 1

Piketty's Proposal

His proposal can be easily derived from his two fundamental laws of capitalism. The first law is an accounting expression which necessarily holds at any point in time and it is expressed by

$$\alpha = r\beta. \tag{1.1}$$

This expression tells us that the capital's share of income, α, is equal to the product of the rate of return on capital, r, and the capital/income ratio, β. The total income, Y, is equal to the capital income, C, plus the labor income, L; therefore $\alpha = \frac{C}{(C+L)}$, and $\beta = \frac{K}{Y}$, where K is the capital stock, whose usage produces the capital income C.

The second law is an economic relationship which requires the passage of time (decades) to realize itself. It is a condition of what is known as the stationary state, which is nothing else than the equilibrium which the economy must necessarily reach in the long run. This law according to Piketty comes from Harrod and Solow growth models but, as we will show, there are crucial differences. This law is expressed by

$$\beta = \frac{s}{g}, \tag{1.2}$$

which tells us that β, the capital/income ratio, is equal to the savings rate, s, divided by the rate of growth of the economy, g. The savings rate, s, is equal to the total savings, S, divided by the total income Y. The rate of economic growth, g, is obtained by multiplying the population growth rate by the per capita income growth rate. Piketty presents all the variables in net terms. Putting together (1.1) and (1.2) we obtain:

$$\frac{\alpha}{r} = \beta = \frac{s}{g}. \tag{1.3}$$

Piketty's capitalist accumulation process maintains relatively constant s and r. Therefore when g falls, with s relatively constant, β goes up; and with r relatively constant, when β goes up α goes up. Therefore a fall on g, due to a fall either in the rate of growth of the population or in the product per capita, implies that both the capital income/ratio, β, and the capital's share, α, go up. And with a wealth distribution favouring the high classes, understood as the richest 1% or 10%, the consequence of α going up is that the income of the high classes goes up in relationship to the rest of the society and the income distribution worsens.

Note that (1.3) defines a stationary state, the necessary equilibrium to be reached in the long run, which in the real world could imply decades. This expression is useful to understand what happens in the long run when g falls; which implies the motion of the economy from one stationary state with a higher g to another one with lower g. A simple way to conceive a stationary state is to imagine an economy which saves 10% of income, produces an income of 100 and grows annually at 2%; the question is: Which should be the value of β in this stationary state? Since a stationary state implies that the value of β must be permanent, β must grow at the same rate as income, at 2%. If savings are 10 and they are equal to 2%, then the capital stock necessarily must be equal to 500, and β is equal to 5.

Piketty's forecast for the second half of the twenty-first century is based on the previously described process. He assumes that g falls to 1.5% and, with s relatively stable at 10%, β will be, in the stationary state, equal to 667%. And with r relatively stable in 4.3%; α will be 29% and the the labor income share equals 71%. The increase in α, given a pronounced wealth ownership concentration, implies an income concentration in favor of the richest 1% or 10%. Finally, the greater the income of the high classes, the higher the inheritance flows; this tendency is strengthened due to the fact that a lower demographic growth implies less descendants per family and a higher inheritance per each one. A higher inheritance flow implies the rapid growth of the renter's class and threatens the basic values of the developed societies, which consider themselves meritocracies.

In the previously described process there are three key variables whose behaviour defines Piketty's forecast: the fall in g and the relative stability of s and r. In particular, with s and r relatively stable, the concentration of income and the increase in the inheritance flow will be higher the lower g falls in relationship to r. The process depends crucially on $r-g$. The higher r in relationship to g, the more pronounced the high class' accumulative capacity in relationship to the rest of the economy. For Piketty, institutions must preclude the consequences that he heralds, thus as α goes up they must introduce a global tax on capital; since finally what counts for the income distribution is the r after taxes. One of the benefits of the global tax would be to finish with the anonymity of the capital that flies to fiscal paradises, another benefit is to gain transparency on inheritance and income distribution statistics.

In what follows we will focus on the dynamics of the three key variables in the process: the rate of return to capital r, the savings rate s, and the rate of growth of the economy g. Such dynamics will be analyzed both theoretically and empirically.

Chapter 2

The dynamics of r

The rate of return of capital, r, is measured empirically in national accounts. It is the ex post realized r. This historical r is given by economic influences as well as by institutional factors. Economically this r has two main contradictory influences, on the one hand there is the law of decreasing returns which says that when capital increases, r must fall; on the other hand there is technological development which shifts the production function and which can allow r to remain high, or even to increase when capital goes up. Observe however that the technology of relevance is only that which is capital-incorporated. Institutionally r is the consequence of power relations which manifest themselves in specific policies, for example in the twenty-first century there are two tendencies: the statist policies consequence of the two wars and the neoliberal policies which start in the 80s. Independently of tax raises or reductions, the salary policy, for example, is critical. Economically if r stays high, when β goes up, it means that the capital-incorporated technological development is more powerful than the decreasing returns. Politically r can be defined by the relative power of the social classes. In particular, in an autocratic society, the rent is not necessarily due to market conditions; and even in democratic societies, the relative power of the social classes can influence r in a significant way.

In economic theory the discussion around the dynamics of r centres in the relative strength of the diminishing returns versus technological development. If we maintain s relatively constant, then in (1.3) when g goes down β goes up, and then if α goes up or not will depend on whether r remains relatively constant or not. But what does it mean that r remains high enough, despite β increases, so that $r - g$ remains also elevated? It means that capital, in spite of its increased size, remains productive. It means that the elasticity between capital and labor, σ, is high. Conceptually in a constant elasticity of substitution production function, this means that σ is greater than one. Since the elasticity between α and β, $\sigma_{\alpha\beta}$, is given by $1 - 1/\sigma$, in general if $\sigma > 1$, $\sigma_{\alpha\beta}$ will be positive. Which means that if β goes up, α also goes up. Note that if σ goes to infinity, it means that capital is a perfect substitute of labor, a fully robotized economy. Piketty and Zucman (2014) infer that, given the fact that empirically from 1970 to 2010 both β and α go up, then $\sigma > 1$; they estimate σ in the range of 1.2 to 1.6—Piketty (2014) changes the range to 1.3 to 1.6. But such inference has been challenged by Rognlie (2014).

The discussion between Rognlie (2014) and Piketty and Zucman (2014) centres in the 1970–2010 statistics of the eight main developed countries. The empirical data shown by Piketty and Zucman for this period are as follows: 1) β has increased from 200-300%, characteristic of the 1970s, to 400-600% recently. This result has to be decomposed into volume increases due to savings and relative price effects due to capital gains or losses; 2) α is more difficult to estimate, but it seems to have increased from the range of 15 to 20% to the range of 25 to 30%. 3) Savings rates have been different in diverse countries. The empirical facts are presented in Table 2.1.

Table 2.1: Empirical facts 1970–2010

Country	β_{1970} (%)	β_{2010} (%)	% of $\Delta\beta$ explained by housing	g (%)	Population growth rate (%)	Real growth rate of per capita national income (%)	s (%)	g_{ws} (%)	g_{wc} (%)	g_w (%)
U.S.	399	456	72	2.8	1.0	1.8	7.7	2.1	0.8	3.0
Japan	356	548	46	2.5	0.5	2.0	14.6	3.1	0.8	3.9
Germany	305	377	157	2.0	0.2	1.8	12.2	3.1	−0.4	2.7
France	340	618	96	2.2	0.6	1.6	11.1	2.7	0.9	3.6
U.K.	359	548	107	2.2	0.3	1.9	7.3	1.5	2.0	3.5
Italy	247	640	71	1.9	0.3	1.6	15.0	2.6	1.5	4.1
Canada	325	422	104	2.8	1.1	1.7	12.1	3.4	0.4	3.8
Australia	410	655	79	3.2	1.4	1.7	9.9	2.5	1.6	4.2

Source: Piketty and Zucman (2014). The first and second columns come from these authors' Table II; they show the domestic capital/national income ratio (remember that domestic capital is equal to national wealth minus net foreign capital). Column 3 is estimated based on their Table II and refers to the percentage of the difference of the first and second columns explained by housing. Columns 4–7 come from their Table III; g is the real growth rate of national income, and s is the net private saving rate. Columns 8–10 come from their Table V; g_w is the real growth rate of national wealth (note that for all countries national wealth grows faster than national income), g_{ws} is the savings-induced wealth growth rate and g_{wc} is the capital gains-induced wealth growth rate.

2.1 Piketty and Zucman's explanation

According to Piketty and Zucman (2014), the β variations in the short run are explained by the price effect (g_{wc} in Table 2.1); but in the long run the volume effect almost exclusively predominates (g_{ws} in Table 2.1). Therefore, during 1970–2010, 43% of the β increase is explained by a price effect; but in the long run, 1870 to 2010, the increase in β is mostly uniquely explained by the second fundamental law of capitalism. And going forward, with s relatively stable, β is mainly explained by the fall in g. Because in the long run the price effect is irrelevant, it follows that the long run is adequately explained by one-good growth models, or in general by any model where capital goods prices move at the same pace than consumer goods prices. The co-movement of α and β implies that the elasticity between capital and labor is greater than one. These authors, as we mentioned, estimate σ^{net} to be around 1.5, or between 1.2 and 1.6.

2.2 The Problems of Piketty and Zucman's explanation

Solow (2014), in his very positive comment on Piketty (2014), mentions that there is certain level of confusion between the definitions of capital and wealth; but he does not go deeper, and, as we will argue, he should have done so, because this seems to be the main problem with Pikkety and Zucman's explanation.

The inconvenience of defining capital as wealth has been discussed by Weil (2015). The problem resides in the fact that for Pikkety and Zucman, wealth and capital are identical. Particularly, Piketty defines capital "as the total market value of everything owned by the residents and government of a given country at a given point in time, provided that it can be traded on some market" (see Piketty, 2014, p. 48). Therefore, national wealth = national capital = domestic capital + net foreign capital. Capital does not include human capital, but it does include physical capital such as: land, housing, buildings, infrastructure, equipment and other forms of physical capital; and also immaterial capital such as patents and intellectual property. The capital income, C, and the rate of return of capital, r, then include "rents, profits, dividends, interest, royalties, etc., excluding interest on public debt (*remember these are both an asset and a liability, therefore at the national level they wash out*), before taxes" (2014, pp. 201-203; italics added).

In economic theory, capital is an input of production subject to the law of diminishing returns, and it is everything in the production function which is not labor. The fundamental characteristic of capital is that it is used to produce. Capital is about quantities, not prices. Therefore, any attempt to measure capital must take away price effects. Housing is one of the ways to accumulate wealth, and since houses are needed in a productive economy, housing must also be considered to a large extent as capital. But there is a fine distinction to be made as to which proportion of saving in housing is really capital and which is not. Because of its peculiar characteristics, it is necessary to analyze housing independently of the rest of capital. In particular the price of housing incorporates the price of the land on which it stands. And land is clearly different to the rest of capital. It is not reproducible and as a consequence it can present relative scarcities, which could increase its real price. Land does not depreciate, it appreciates. But lets look specifically why Piketty's definition of capital is problematic for the interpretation he makes of the data he presents.

2.3 The discussion about capital gains and the rise in the price of land

As we previously mentioned capital is about quantities, hence we need to remove price effects. Piketty and Zucman do it by differentiating volume effects due to savings from capital gains or losses. In this context, it becomes critical how much of the β increase is only due to price effects. The discussion is how to measure capital gains; and it is related as to how to better measure β, if at market prices or at book value. The results are quite different. Table 2.2 shows the outcome. If β is measured at market value, β_{mv}, capital gains explain between 43% and 55% of the β increase; if β is measured at book value, β_{bv}, capital gains explain -135%.

Table 2.2: Variation rate of β due to capital gains from 1970 to 2010

Piketty & Zucman. S corrected by R&D, β_{mv}. Best estimate.*	43%
Piketty & Zucman. S corrected by R&D, β_{mv}. NBER estimate.[†]	50–60%
Rognlie. S without R&D, β_{mv}.[‡]	84%
Rognlie. S does not require correction, β_{bv}.[‡]	−135%

Sources:
*Piketty and Zucman (2014), see the online Appendix Table A99 available at
`http://piketty.pse.ens.fr/en/capitalisback`.
[†]Piketty and Zucman (2014), see online section A.5.2 of the Data Appendix available
at `http://piketty.pse.ens.fr/en/capitalisback`.
[‡]Rognlie (2014).

If we measure β at market values we must correct savings, S, as it appears in national accounts due to the fact that it does not include research and development (R&D) expenditures, which are included in the market value of β. If we do not do this correction capital gains explain 84% of the β movement, but the correction is required. The problem is how to estimate R&D expenditures. The National Bureau of Economic Research (NBER) estimates 1% of the gross domestic product (GDP) for the United States, Piketty and Zucman using this estimate calculate that capital gains explain between 50 and 60% of the β movements. They however, argue that the NBER estimate is too low, and they introduced a new estimate of 2%, with which capital gains only explain 43%.

If we measure β at book value there is no need to correct savings because R&D expenditures are not included in book values. Rognlie (2014), surprisingly, shows that with β measured at book value, capital gains account for −135% of the β movements.[1] Which means, that if β is measured at book value, for the eight countries shown in Piketty and Zucman (2014), the average β actually decreases between 1970 and 2010.

Looking at the fact that capital gains explain more than 100% of the β movements, Rognlie argues that it must be due to an increase in the real price of land. The scarcity of critical land must have increased its price; and it is this price increase what explains the increases in β. Therefore, he argues, there is not a secular tendency for β to go up.

2.4   The role of housing

As we pointed out, what allows for α to go up when β goes up is the relative rigidity of r. Such rigidity is due to a high elasticity of substitution between capital and labor, σ. Empirically, if both α and β go up it seems to imply that σ must be greater than 1. But what happens if we decompose wealth in two components, housing and the rest? Such decomposition is particularly relevant because of two reasons: 1) the fast technological development, which could oppose the law of decreasing returns, does not occur in housing, 2) most of the β increase in developed countries is due to housing. The problem of housing capital has been noted also by Auerbach and Hassett (2015), Rognlie (2014) and Rognlie (2015).

---

[1]Capital gains are greater using book values since for the selected countries Tobin's q is less than 1,(see Table 2.5).

Rognlie makes the decomposition previously discussed. The first observation is that housing explains 80% of the β increase in the period 1970–2010, Rognlie (2014, p. 16). Once we eliminate housing, he estimates, there is only a small increase in β and a small decrease in α, which means $\sigma < 1$, and a lower r. Why when we include housing σ is greater than one, and when we exclude it σ is less than one? The basic reason argued by Rognlie, as we mentioned before, is that the real price of land has risen, and therefore the one-good model used by Piketty and Zucman becomes inadequate. When the price of land goes up, because its consumption is inelastic, the proportion of income spent in housing goes up, and this is the main cause of the observed increases in β. To estimate σ from the co-movement of α and β is not possible whenever the real price of capital moves differently than the price of consumption goods—the case of land. Rognlie has argued that the co-movement observed between α and β, during 1970–2010, is due to the increase in the price of land; that is why, he says, that a better title for Piketty's book would have been Housing in the Twenty-First Century.

Rognlie shows that if g falls, for example from 3% to 1.5%, $r - g$ falls rapidly. Only if we were out of Piketty's world, with s being a positive function of g, it would be possible that when g falls, as s also falls, $r - g$ could remain high. But in such a world β would go up much less than what Piketty assumes—see the next section about the dynamics of savings.

The discussion between Rognlie and Piketty-Zucman has great relevance, because if the secular tendency of β to increase cannot be shown for 1970–2010, which is the period for which we have solid national accounts, Pikkety's explanation of the dynamics of capitalism is in trouble.

One more piece of evidence that seems to confirm the argument that what explains the $\sigma > 1$, argued by Pikety and Zucman, is the rise in housing prices is the article by Bonnet et al. (2014). This article shows that if we substitute the real price of housing for the price that corresponds to the discounted value of the future rental flow that they represent, using actual rents as an indicator, β (including housing at this new calculated price) only goes up moderately.[2] This means that housing is overvalued and the fact that rents have not gone up as much as housing prices questions that today housing prices are sustainable in the long run. This is an additional question mark to the thesis that Capital is Back. Low rents in relation to housing prices (see Table 2.4) indicate overvaluation and signals that what can be behind Piketty's increase in β is the recent housing boom in the developed countries.

The IMF Global Housing Watch shows that in 2010 housing overvaluation is greater in France and the U. K., and very small in the U. S., while there is undervaluation in Germany. They argue that housing prices were overvalued 23% in 2010 in relationship to 2000. Similar results can be obtained analyzing *The Economist* data of house prices against rents for the same period (visit `http://www.economist.com/blogs/dailychart/2011/11/global-house-prices`).

Table 2.3 shows the percentage increase—2010 compared to 1970—in β, and how it is

---

[2]The mentioned authors argue that even the distributional consequences of the β increases mentioned by Piketty are questionable, since rents are finally the income of those renting their properties as well as of those living in them. Therefore distributional effects will only be related to the difficulty of becoming a house owner and to the capacity of those owning a house of selling it at an overvalued price and getting an extraordinary benefit.

explained by housing and non-housing β, denoted by β_h and β_{nh} respectively, for the seven major developed economies. And Table 2.4 shows housing prices comparing 1975 to 2010 in real terms as well as against rents and against average income. In France and the United Kingdom, where houses are significantly overvalued, the percentage increase in total β was very high and it is more than totally explained by housing. In Australia and Canada houses are also significantly overvalued and the % total β increase is as high or higher than in the U.K.; in Australia almost all of the percentage increase in β is explained by housing, while in Canada a portion of the increase is due to β_{nh}.

In the U.S., where houses are close to their value, housing also explains more than the percentage increase in total β, but the β increase was very moderate. In Germany housing is undervalued, therefore the percentage increase in total β, which is more than fully explained by housing, represents real savings related to the reconstruction of East Germany. This reconstruction of East Germany will later on explain, in Table 3.2, why savings remain high for Germany despite the fall in the rate of growth of the economy. In Japan most of the total β increase is due to non-housing and the part due to housing is also related to real savings because houses are undervalued. These two facts will explain later on, in Table 2.5, why Japan is the only country where there is an inverse relationship between α increases and total β increases at market value.

Table 2.3: Percentage increase in β explained by β_h and β_{nh} from 1970 to 2010

	U.S.	U.K.	France	Germany	Japan	Canada	Australia
β increase (%)	7	45	73	33	71	45	50
Explained by β_h (%)	10	55	76	34	25	35	49
Explained by β_{nh} (%)	−3	−10	−3	−1	46	10	1

Source: Author's calculations based on Appendix Tables A1 and A16 of Piketty and Zucman (2014), available at `http://piketty.pse.ens.fr/en/capitalisback`. The increase explained by β_{nh} is calculated based on these tables.

Table 2.4: Housing prices 1975–2010

	U.S.	U.K.	France	Germany	Japan	Canada	Australia
In real terms*	120.9	205.2	230.5	85.5	89.9	211.8	279.1
Against rents†	96.4	137.2	137.0	76.9	66.6	158.3	157.8
Against average income†	84.3	118.9	130.5	75.6	68.8	125.1	133.3

Source: *The Economist* house-price index available at `http://www.economist.com/blogs/dailychart/2011/11/global-house-prices`.
*Q4 2010 vs. Q1 1975 (= 100).
†Q4 2010 vs Long-term average (= 100).

2.5 Price effects and speculative waves

Capital must be productive and it includes housing when it is productive. But housing does not behave like the rest of capital, it can have long speculative waves which will not only overvalue housing—which will show in capital gains—but also will produce over-construction—which will be reflected in more savings. Both components will increase β_h and the total β. These long waves will increase wealth and may have repercussions in the capital income share, α. But such waves cannot be the base of a long-run forecast, because the high prices and the over-construction will have an end as they build the forces of their own destruction. Thus, while housing can influence the growth of β in the medium term, it will not be a decisive factor in the long run.

Moreover, speculative housing waves are not unique in influencing β in the medium term, there are other effects which need to be discussed; amongst them, the relationship between β_{bv} and β_{mv}. Looking at the historical data of the main developed countries we find that from 1970 to 2010 when α goes up market value national wealth-national income ratio, β_{mv}, also goes up as Piketty argues; but β at book value, β_{bv}, goes down both in the U.S. and in the U.K. (See Table 2.5). This implies that in these countries the positive relationship between α and β that Piketty finds is partially due to the fact that the main stock markets have been going up since 1970, which has occationed that β_{mv} get closer to β_{bv}; in other words the Tobin's q ratios have been going up. They have been going up particularly in the U.S. and the U.K. (see Table 2.5). Therefore, β_{mv} increases, despite the fact that β_{bv} is decreasing, only due to the fact that β_{mv} gets closer to β_{bv}.

What does it mean that β_{mv} gets closer to β_{bv}? When the market value gets closer to the book value, or even exceeds it, it means that share holders are more confident as to the managerial usage of assets and therefore stock owners discount the market price less in relationship to its book value. But this process has nothing to do with productivity. The physical and intellectual company capital does not go up when β_{mv} gets closer to β_{bv}; companies are the same, we have only a price effect as stock owners decide to value more the stocks. This price effect again cannot be the base of a long run forecast, because it has its own limits as to how far it can go. In order to avoid the medium-term noise produced by this price effect, and to better describe the long-term relation between α and β, it is better to compare α, with β_{bv}.

There is a long discussion in economics regarding the usefulness of β_{mv} vs. β_{bv}. There is no doubt that measuring capital at market prices has many advantages. Market prices take into account not only a view of the future through the discount rate used to value future income, but they also take into account present information in many variables—for example proven oil reserves. And market prices also include adequately intangible assets like research and development. For the previous reasons book value is not a good substitute for market value. However, market value is neither a good substitute of book value. They just provide different information, and both are useful. Market value has the problem that asset markets are very volatile. Book value presents a better view of the quantity of inputs in a production function; it allows us to take away the price effects.

In a stationary state there cannot be differences between the two measures, because in a stationary state there is no uncertainty about the future. This is the reason that we can estimate the stationary value of β given data on the growth rate of income and on the savings rate. If some of the capital became unproductive then the value of β couldn't be defined because it would not be permanent any longer. An stationary state means a repetitive economy, therefore it would make no sense in such an economy to book assets unless they are productive.

Book values and market values must be aligned in the very long run because otherwise, why to book assets that will not become productive? The trial and error and the constant innovation in real markets, doesn't take away the fact that economic agents optimize and therefore will only book those assets that they believe will be productive. Basic theory tells us that in the very long run book values and market values must be aligned. In fact this is the very meaning of a stationary state.

Table 2.5: α and β relationships: Average of 1991–2010 /Average of 1971–1990 (%)

Country	α_{total}	β_{mv}	β_{bv}	α_{nh}	β_{nhmv}	β_{nhbv}	Tobin's q	$\beta_{mv} - \beta_{bv}$
U.S.	12.23	11.58	−5.11	6.17	8.76	−16.60	21.10	16.69
U.K.	22.31	15.02	−17.70	15.32	−2.83	−43.44	19.56	32.73
France	30.28	20.56	18.23	15.94	−9.18	−4.74	7.72	2.33
Germany	32.26	11.62	8.22	34.58[a]	−5.14	−3.01	13.99	3.40
Japan	−3.73	20.58	15.31	−12.55	26.49	16.93	8.85	5.26
Canada	14.74	18.36	2.65	9.17	8.89	−9.20	9.04	15.71
Australia	8.11	21.65	10.10	0.19	−0.77	−12.06	14.15[c]	11.55
Weighted Average	14.18	14.50	1.16	4.57[b]	7.37	−10.60	16.62[d]	–

Sources: Appendix Tables of Piketty and Zucman (2014), available at http://piketty.pse.ens.fr/en/capitalisback. Here α_{total} is the capital share in factor-price national income, comes from Table A48b. β_{mv} is the market value national wealth/national income ratio, Table A1. β_{bv} is the book value national wealth/national income ratio, Table A12. α_{nh} is non-housing capital share in factor price national income, is estimated from Table A48b minus (A144 × A16); for Germany α_{nh} appears as not available because Table A144 starts in 1990 for this country and therefore calculating the needed change is not possible. β_{nhmv} is the non-housing national wealth at market value/national income ratio, is estimated from Tables A1 minus A16. β_{nhbv} is the non-housing national wealth at book value/national income ratio, is estimated from Tables A12 minus A16. Weighted Average is obtained using the percentage that each country represents in the sum of all for the year 2010, using as reference national income PPP (purchasing power parity) at constant 2011 international dollars. Housing only includes the housing wealth of households and excludes residential real estate held by governments and corporations. Tobin's q ratios in the table are average q's which are equal to: (market value of outstanding equities + market value of debt liabilities)/book value of assets.

[a] For Germany data is not really valid because data in Table A144 starts only in 1990, therefore it is comparing only 1990 to the average 1991–2010. For France data in Table A144 starts in 1979.
[b] Does not include Germany; if it is included the value is 7.88.
[c] For Australia the comparison is not valid because there are no data from 1971 to 1989, therefore it is comparing only 1990 to the average 1991–2010.
[d] Australia is not included, if it is included the data is 16.56.

Table 2.5 shows that national wealth β at market value, increased for all the countries, and, as Piketty has argued, there is a positive relationship with the share of capital in national income, α; except for Japan where the relationship is negative. However, it can be seen, that just by measuring β at book value, the relationship becomes, as we mentioned previously, negative for the U.S. and the U.K.. Moreover, once we remove housing, and we continue valuing national capital β at book value, there is no longer a positive relationship between β and α as Piketty assumes; it is negative for all the countries. The results shown in Table 2.5, as we will see, are compatible with the literature on the elasticity of substitution between capital and labor, σ.

Using Tables 2.3, 2.4 and 2.5, let us better explain the situation in each particular country. In the U.S. housing explains more than the increase in total β and therefore the positive relationship between α and β at market value emphasized by Piketty. The price effect between market value and book value is powerful, $\beta_{mv} - \beta_{bv} = 16.69$. Therefore β_{bv} is inversely related to α. Housing is not significantly overvalued (see Table 2.4); therefore, the increase in α is mostly due to real housing wealth, which may reflect some speculative over-construction, but the percentage increase in total β is small. In principle since the % explained by β_{nh} is negative in Table 2.3, one would expect β_{nhmv} in Table 2.5 to go down, but it actually increases—this is due to the additional effect of the stocks market value getting closer to their book value. As we can see the Tobin's q average between the two periods increases the most in the U.S. (see Table 2.5), and, as we mentioned, what is even more significant, $\beta_{mv} - \beta_{bv}$ is very high. But if we remove this price effect we find that β_{nhbv} is inversely related to both α_{total} and α_{nh} (see Table 2.5).

In the U.K., again housing explains more than the β increase and therefore the positive relation between α and β_{mv}. In the U.K. the price effect between market values and book values is the strongest, $\beta_{mv} - \beta_{bv} = 32.73$. Therefore β_{bv} is powerfully inversely related to α. Like the U.S., the increase in β is very well explained by housing, but since houses are significantly overvalued the increase in β is substantial (see Table 2.3). The percentage explained by non-housing in the U.K. is actually the most negative, therefore one would expect for β_{nh} at market value to go down and it actually does, but not by much because it is also influenced by the very powerful price effect between market values and book values. The U.K. also has a very significant increase in Tobin's q, and it has the highest difference between β_{mv} and β_{bv} which shows the very powerful price effect mentioned. Once this price effect is removed and we value non-housing β at book value then the decrease is notoriously high. β_{nhbv} is inversely related, like in all the countries, both to α_{total} and to α_{nh}.

In France again β_h explains more than 100% of the β increase and therefore the positive relation between α and β_{mv}. In France houses are the most overvalued and the β increase is also the highest. And like in the U.S. and the U.K., the total percentage increase of β explained by β_{nh} is negative therefore one should expect β_{nhmv} to go down, and it actually does significantly because the price effect between market values and book values is very small in France, $\beta_{mv} - \beta_{bv}$ is only 2.33. Again β_{nhbv} is inversely related to α and to α_{nh}.

In Germany housing explains again more than the total β increase, and therefore the positive relation between α and β. But houses are undervalued, therefore the total β increase is substantially lower than in all the other countries except the U.S.. Housing in Germany is related to real housing construction due to the reconstruction of East Germany. Again the percentage explained by non-housing is negative, therefore one would expect β_{nh} to go down, and it does because the price effect in Germany related to market value vs. book value is small, $\beta_{mv} - \beta_{bv} = 3.40$. β_{nhbv} again is inversely related to α_{total} and to α_{nh}.

In Japan housing only explains partially the total β increase, which is mostly explained by non-housing β. Also the price effect related to market value vs. book value is small, Japan has a low Tobin's q and a $\beta_{mv} - \beta_{bv}$ equal only to 5.62. Moreover, housing in Japan is undervalued. Therefore, diminishing returns related to the significant increase in total β prevail in the whole wealth and there is an inverse relationship between α and β_{mv}. There is of course also an inverse relationship between all the other measures of β (β_{bv}, β_{nhmv} and β_{nhbv}) and the two measures of capital income share, α_{total} and α_{nh}. Japan actually exemplifies what happens to an economy when the speculative housing wave is over and in which housing increases are due to real construction, and where the price effects between β_{mv} and β_{bv} are small, as theory would suggest, the relationship between β_{mv} and α is negative due to the diminishing returns that predominate in all the wealth.

In Canada housing is significantly overvalued and the total β increase is explained mostly by housing, which explains the positive relationship between β_{mv} and α. But the percentage explained by non-housing is positive and significant, therefore one would expect for β_{nhmv} to go up and it does, partially due to this effect and the high effect of market values vs. book values, $\beta_{mv} - \beta_{bv} = 15.71$. But once we remove the price effect β_{nhbv} will inversely relate, like in all cases to α and to α_{nh}.

Finally, in Australia housing is the most overvalued and it explains almost all of the β increase and the positive relation between β_{mv} and α. Once we remove housing, β_{nhmv} goes down but only minimally because there's is a significant price effect, $\beta_{mv} - \beta_{bv} = 11.55$. Once we remove the price effect β_{nhbv} goes down and is inversely related to both α and α_{nh}.

In summary: the positive relationship between α and β_{mv} is due to housing and price effects between market value and book value wealth. If we remove the price effects, both the U.S. and the U.K. show a negative relationship between α and β_{bv}. If we remove housing the U.K., France, Germany and Australia show an inverse relationship between β_{nhmv} and α. If we remove both housing and the price effects all the contries show an inverse relation between β_{nhbv} and both α and α_{nh}.

2.6 The elasticity between capital and labor

Everything seems to indicate that the gross elasticity of substitution between capital and labor, σ (previously denoted as σ^{gross}), is less than 1.25. Chirinko and Mallick (2014) make a review on the literature estimating σ concluding that the best range estimate is 0.40–0.60. It is worth mentioning that the highest σ, found in aggregate investment data, is 1.59 and corresponds to computers; and that the equipment σ, in panel data, is 0.93. Mallick (2007) estimates worldwide σ in 0.338, see also Mallick (2012). This author corroborates the de la Grandville hypothesis, and shows that there is a positive correlation between g and σ. But anyway the highest σ which corresponds to East Asia is only 0.737. Chirinko and Mallick (2014) conclude that their best estimate is 0.406. They also estimate σ for heterogeneous industries and amongst their results we find agriculture $\sigma = 0.289$, construction $\sigma = 0.41$, machinery $\sigma = 0.483$, electrical machinery $\sigma = 0.486$. The highest σ corresponds to finance, insurance and real estate and it is of 1.16. These authors analyze the possibility that σ may rise in the future as economies develop, and they concentrate on a specific subset of industries that they call the post-industrial economy. But even if this were to happen the σ corresponding to the mentioned specific subset of industries is only 0.857. Oberfield and Raval (2014) argue that even taking into account increases due to cross sector elasticity, the manufacturing sector σ in the United States would not be higher than 0.7; and for the manufacturing sectors of some other countries the corresponding value will be $\sigma = 0.84$ for Chile and Colombia, and $\sigma = 1.11$ for India. Few authors in the past, who represent a minority, have argued that in the long run $\sigma = 1$, see Jones (2005). And finally Karabarbounis and Neiman (2014) focus in long-term sequences, variation amongst sectors and use many industries and countries estimating $\sigma = 1.25$. In summary, taking into account Piketty's argument that σ may rise in the long run,

Table 2.6: σ^{gross}, σ^{net}, $\sigma_{\alpha\beta}$, α and r

	σ^{gross}					
σ^{gross}	0.406	0.857	1.25	1.61	4.00	100 000
σ^{net}	0.252	0.532	0.776	1.00	2.484	62 089.173
$\sigma_{\alpha\beta}$	-2.967	-0.879	-0.288	0.00	0.597	1.0
	$\beta_2/\beta_1 = 1.52$ and $\alpha_1 = 18.92\%$					
$\alpha_2(\%)$	0.0	10.35	16.11	18.92	24.74	28.67
$r_2\ (\%)$	-1.5	1.55	2.42	2.84	3.71	4.30

$\sigma_{\alpha\beta}$ is the elasticity of substitution between α and β, given by $1 - \frac{1}{\sigma^{net}}$. Here β_2 is 667%, the value of β in Piketty's forecast for 2100, and β_1 is 440%, corresponding to the observed β in 2010. Then α_1 is obtained multiplying $r = 0.043$ by β_1. α_2 in terms of $\sigma^{\alpha\beta}$ is given by $\alpha_2 = \left(\frac{\beta_2}{\beta_1} - 1\right)\alpha_1\sigma_{\alpha\beta} + \alpha_1$. Finally $r_2 = \frac{\alpha_2}{\beta_2}$.

one could expect for σ to be higher than the 0.406 estimated by Chirinko and Mallick (2014); but we have two specific responses as to the range at which σ may belong in the future— Chirinko and Mallick (2014) and Karabarbounis and Neiman (2014). Therefore σ most likely will be in the range of 0.857 to 1.25.

Rognlie (2014) shows that $\sigma^{net} = \sigma^{gross} \cdot \left(\frac{r^{gross} - \delta}{r^{gross}}\right) \cdot \left(\frac{1}{1 - \frac{\delta K}{\text{GNI}}}\right)$, and using U.S. data and GDP instead of gross national income (GNI), he also shows that $\sigma^{net} \approx 0.66\sigma^{gross}$. Using the 1990–2010 world statistics from the World Bank, $\left(\frac{s_b}{\text{GNI}}\right) - \left(\frac{s_n}{\text{GNI}}\right) = \frac{\delta K}{\text{GNI}} = 0.1315$. And since $\frac{\delta K}{K} = \delta = \frac{\frac{1}{\beta}\left(\frac{\delta K}{\text{GNI}}\right)}{\left(1 - \frac{\delta K}{\text{GNI}}\right)}$, using the average $\beta = 412\%$ for 1990–2010, then we have that $\delta = 0.0367$. Therefore using $r^{gross} - \delta = 0.043$, from Piketty (2014, Supplemental Table S6.2, Excel version), we obtain $r^{gross} = 0.043 + 0.0367 = 0.0797$; $1 - \frac{\delta K}{\text{GNI}} = 1 - 0.1315 = 0.8685$. And $\sigma^{net} \approx 0.62\sigma^{gross}$. Table 2.6 shows the σ^{net} corresponding to six values of σ^{gross}: 1) Chirinko and Mallick (2014) best estimate of 0.406; 2) the previous authors long-run estimate of 0.857; 3) Karabarbounis and Neiman (2014) long-run estimate of 1.25; 4) the equilibrium value of 1.61 below which the α-β relation is negative and above which it is positive[3]; 5) the value of 4 argued by Rognlie as needed to explain the co-movement between α and β from 1970 to 2010; 6) the value 100,000 introduced only to show that at very high values of σ^{gross}, the percentage change in α is identical to the percentage change in β. This case is interesting because it is similar to Piketty (2014)'s forecast for the second half of the twenty-first century.

Table 2.6 allows us to reach two conclusions:

1. As previously mentioned, Piketty and Zucman have argued that the co-movement between α and β from 1970 to 2010 is compatible with a σ of around 1.5, but since they refer to net elasticity in reality their 1.5 means a σ^{gross} of around 2.42. Rognlie argues

---

[3]The formula giving the percentage change of α is $[1 - (1/0.62089\sigma^{gross})] \times (\beta_2/\beta_1 - 1)$. Notice that the first term in this expression becomes zero when $\sigma^{gross} = 1.61$, and therefore α does not change independently of the value of β_2/β_1. Besides, notice that for σ^{gross} less than 1.61 the first term is negative, therefore the change in α will be inversely related to the change in β. Only when the value of σ^{gross} is greater than 1.61 the change in α has the same sign as the change in β.

that the explanation of the co-movement between α and β will require a gross σ^{gross} of around 4. But even the 2.42 is incompatible with the literature estimate of σ^{gross}, therefore something else, which is not the σ, must be explaining such co-movement. As we have argued, that something is the rise in the price of land associated with the housing boom and the price effect between β_{mv} and β_{bv}, as investors value stocks closer to their book value.

2. Piketty in his 2014 forecasts maintains r before taxes at the same level it had from 1990 to 2010, despite the fact that private wealth β changes from 440% in 2010 (the average was 420%) to 667% in 2100, an increase of 52%.[4] This will imply an almost infinite σ between capital and labor.

Is there any basis for Piketty (2014)'s forecast? The co-movement shown between α and β in the weighted averages of columns 1 and 2 in Table 2.5, indicates that α and β almost move together as far as the average of these two periods is concerned. This implies an extremely high simple σ^{net} between the average of the two periods of 45.3125, and seems to provide a basis for Piketty's forecast of a relatively rigid r, but such σ^{net} corresponds to a $\sigma^{gross} = 73.085$, which is totally out of bounds of the empirical studies on σ^{gross}.[5] An extremely high σ would mean a robot society where machines can fully substitute human beings, nobody believes on it as a serious possibility and the empirical evidence suggests that $0.857 < \sigma^{gross} < 1.25$. The co-movement of α and β, as we have argued, is due to other factors, the increase in the real price of land related to the housing boom and the price effects between β_{mv} and β_{bv}. Therefore, such co-movement cannot provide an adequate basis for a long-run forecast. In fact, if we take away housing and we value wealth at book value the implied simple σ^{net} between the two periods, weighted averages of columns four and six in Table 2.5, is only 0.6987, corresponding to a $\sigma^{gross} = 1.127$, that is within the bounds estimated by the empirical studies.

2.7 What is capital and how to forecast it

If we look at the United States, the most advanced economy in the world, the wealth in average, from 1960 to 2013, takes the following distribution: 55.6% is housing, other real estate is 6.7%, structures, such as highways and others, 15.7%, equipment 11.4%, intellectual property 4.0%, foreign assets 3.1% and inventories 4%.[6] These different segments of wealth have different gross σ's. The highest σ found is in computers 1.59; finance, insurance and real estate 1.16; and equipment 0.93. Notice the small percentage that represent the high technological sectors, and that not even them have a σ higher than the equilibrium value of 1.61. Therefore, there

---

[4] There is no discussion that these are Piketty's assumptions. The reader can look at Figure 10.9 of Piketty (2014, p. 354), at Supplemental Table S6.2 (Excel version) available at `http://piketty.pse.ens.fr/en/capital21c2`, or at our Table 2.8

[5] Simple σ^{net} is the ratio of the relative changes of two variables, given by $\sigma^{net} = \frac{1}{1-\sigma^{\alpha\beta}}$. So, for the first two columns of Table 2.5, $\sigma^{net} = \frac{1}{1-\left(\frac{14.18}{14.50}\right)} = 45.3125$, while for columns 4 and 6, $\sigma^{net} = \frac{1}{1-\left(\frac{4.57}{-10.60}\right)} = 0.6987$.

[6] Data from the Integrated Macro Accounts, Bureau of Economic Analysis, September 2014.

is no way to justify that capital-incorporated technology will have the strength to undermine the diminishing returns that operate in all the capital segments with low σ's.

From a productive technological perspective, as Table 2.6 shows, Piketty's 2014 forecast of a 52% of increase in β relates, at all known empirical estimates, with a fall in α; which shows the strength of the law of decreasing returns—a higher β leads to a higher proportional fall in r. This is consistent with the results found in Table 2.5.

Piketty however, despite his β forecast, has chosen to maintain r high. In fact, Piketty has chosen to maintain r at 4.3%, the same level it had between 1990 and 2010. To verify that this is the case, the reader may want to look at Figure 10.9 in Piketty (2014, p. 354) and also at the Supplemental Table S6.2 (Excel version available at `http://piketty.pse.ens.fr/en/capital21c2`), or alternatively at our Table 2.8. At this point it is convenient to quote Piketty directly: "For the twenty-first century, I have assumed that the value observed in the period 1990–2010 (about 4%) will continue, but this is of course uncertain: there are forces pushing towards a lower return and other forces pushing toward a higher", Piketty (2014, p. 354). The point however, is that if β increases substantially, like in Piketty's forecast, the forces pushing towards a higher rate of return are extremely weak because only a very small portion of wealth may have a higher elasticity than the equilibrium point in Table 2.6 of 1.61. But the forces working towards a reduced r, as β increases substantially, are very strong because almost all of wealth has low elasticity between capital and labor.

Piketty on his forecast was confronted with a dilemma: historically r has remained relatively high, but technologically that is inconsistent with big increases in β as the one he forecasts. He has chosen to forget the productive characteristics of capital and to ignore the strong relationship between β and r given by the empirical estimates of σ. We will argue that such choice is deeply wrong because it ignores the homeostatic dynamics of the markets. It is true that β can increase in the short to medium term due to nonproductive factors—wealth effects due to speculative housing waves and $\beta_{mv} - \beta_{bv}$ price effects—and that r can remain high, but in the long run markets will tend towards homogenizing the r's in the different segments of wealth. Economically we cannot base a long-run forecast neither in a housing boom and an increase of the real price of land, nor in β_{mv} getting closer to β_{bv}. The long-run forecast has to be based in the technological characteristics of production. Because, if we assumed that housing has an r much higher than the productive non-housing segment, then more wealth would go into the housing segment in the long run to equalize the rates of return. Price effects can certainly increase β_{mv} in the short to medium term but they will have to give away in the long run to the productive characteristics of the society. Piketty was wrong in defining capital as wealth without exploring more deeply the consequences. The forecast for the long-run future cannot be based in an r that remains the same, despite the fact that β increases 52%. Either r goes down or β cannot go up. If r goes down, because σ is less than the equilibrium value, then α will go down instead of increasing. If r remains relatively close to its 1990–2010 level then β also has to do the same. In our final conclusion we will argue that what is wrong is the β forecast of Piketty; but at this point it is too early to jump into that argument because we will need the discussion on savings in the following section.

The previous discussion must not be misread as the argument that the distribution of income cannot worsen. In fact, the speculative housing waves and other price effects may deteriorate the income distribution in the short to medium term. And there are all sort of institutional factors that may in real life worsen the income distribution; some that Piketty comments, like the salaries of the supermanagers in the U.S., and some that he does not, like growth, urban, educational and health policies amongst others. There may also be powerful political forces pushing for policies that may deteriorate the income distribution. Therefore, the society has to be always alert. But Piketty's dynamics, which implies that there are powerful long-run economic forces that will necessarily concentrate the income distribution is, as we will show, unsustainable.

2.8   Piketty and Zucman's arguments in relationship to the long run

In Table 2.7 we can appreciate the authors' argument that in the long run the savings rate is predominant over capital gains or losses.

However, their argument that β is coming back to previous levels and that therefore there is a historical "U-shaped curve", does not hold for the United States, which looks more than a straight line than a U-curve (see Table 2.7). In the case of Germany it also does not seem to be a U-shaped curve, β in 2010 in relationship to 1870 is only 0.56. In the United Kingdom and France it would seem that there is the argued U-shaped curve; the same indicator is 0.80 and 0.88 respectively. However, note that in the United Kingdom there is a significant fall up to 1980; $\beta_{1980}/\beta_{1870}$ is only 0.63%. In the case of France $\beta_{1980}/\beta_{1870}$ is only 0.56, and afterwards the U-curve seems also to be confirmed. It is really in the period 1980 to 2010, that a U-curve seems to be confirmed, but this is exactly the period where the speculative housing wave and the β_{mv}-β_{bv} price effect are stronger.

The argument that the previous analysis brings forward is that the data by itself do not show a long-run tendency for β to have a U-curve. In 1970, and even in 1980, there was nothing that suggested that β would necessarily increase.

Table 2.8 presents the data used by Piketty (2014) in figures 10.9 and 10.10. Starting 1820–1913, the rate of growth of the economy substantially accelerates and, as a consequence of new technologies and competition for capital, r goes up, but less than the increase in g; therefore $r - g$ falls in the last three historical periods presented in the table. Exactly the opposite of what would happen in Piketty's forecast. The clue of Piketty's forecast is that r, as β increases substantially, falls less than g. In here there are two conclusions to discuss. In the first place for $r - g$ to grow is not a law of capitalism, in fact from 1820 onwards, according to Piketty, the opposite happened. In the second place, the historical data do not support Piketty's forecast of a relatively rigid r when the economy confronts a substantial decline in g and a substantial increase in β.

It may be true that the historical rate of return of capital was high; Piketty estimates it at 4.5%. And, if it indeed was high, it was probably due to two factors: the scarcity of capital and the relative political power of the capitalists. But if Piketty's forecast of an abrupt increase in β materialized, then r could not be in the future as high as in the past: r would necessarily go down due to decreasing returns.

From the point of view of income distribution the relevant r is the one after taxes. As it can be seen in Table 2.8, $r - g$ after taxes becomes negative in the twentieth century as a result of the aggressive taxes consequence of the wars. As it can be appreciated the r before and after taxes difference is null before 1913, from 1913 to 1950 is 4%, and from 1950 to 2012 is 2.1%; and Piketty's forecast is only of 0.4% for 2012-2050 and zero for 2050-2100. Taxes reflect the relative power of the middle class versus the high class, and it is true that the high class has gained territory since 1980; but in most developed countries taxes have cyclical characteristics, therefore it is likely that the middle class will recover territory again and it is not a good assumption to forecast a heavy decline in taxes: certainly not the zero assumed by Piketty. Besides with very low taxes, how would governments finance themselves?

To finalize this section, let's make a few general remarks. To build r, it is necessary to have statistics of both capital income and capital stock. In relationship to capital income there are solid statistics since the Second World War and efforts of government agencies and academicians to provide much older data. At the world level, however, there is only one consistent database since 1990 in the World Bank data, remember that it is needed to have constant currency international dollars with the same PPP (purchasing power parity). In relationship to capital stock, several countries started serious statistical efforts since the 90's. For example, the United States presents statistics since 1960. However there are not adequate consolidated statistics at the global level. It is true that this is one of the reasons for which Piketty's work is so welcome, he does indeed a serious and professional job to define a comparable capital stock at the world level. He is particularly successful in France, the U.K. and to a large extent in the U.S. But it is also true that many statistics are difficult to consolidate and that their consolidation requires many assumptions. Just to remind the reader in something as simple as the growth of the economy, Maddison and the World Bank

Table 2.7: β and its variation due to savings and capital gains

Period	β_t (%)	β_{t+n} (%)	% of growth induced by savings	% of growth induced by capital gains	β_t (%)	β_{t+n} (%)	% of growth induced by savings	% of growth induced by capital gains
	United States				**France**			
1870–2010	413	431	76	24	689	605	91	9
1870–1910	413	469	68	32	689	747	103	−3
1910–2010	469	431	80	20	747	605	89	11
1910–1950	469	380	82	18	747	261	8	92
1950–1980	380	434	94	6	261	383	80	20
1970–2010	404	431	72	28	351	605	75	25
1980–2010	434	431	58	42	383	605	65	35
	United Kingdom				**Germany**			
1870–2010	656	527	83	17	745	416	128	−28
1870–1910	656	719	79	21	745	637	107	−7
1910–2010	719	527	86	14	637	416	137	−37
1910–1950	719	241	−43	143	637	223	−3	103
1950–1980	241	416	76	24	223	330	108	−8
1970–2010	365	527	42	58	313	416	114	−14
1980–2010	416	527	28	72	330	416	101	−1

Source: Tables V and VII of Piketty and Zucman (2014).

Table 2.8: Piketty's historical data

Period	$r - g$ (b. taxes)	$r - g$ (a. taxes)	r (b. taxes)	r (a. taxes)	g (%)	g (per capita, %)	Population (growth, %.)
0–1000	4.5	4.5	4.5	4.5	0.01	0.00	0.02
1000–1500	4.4	4.4	4.5	4.5	0.14	0.04	0.10
1500–1700	4.3	4.3	4.5	4.5	0.20	0.04	0.16
1700–1820	4.6	4.6	5.1	5.1	0.53	0.07	0.46
1820–1913	3.5	3.5	5.0	5.0	1.49	0.90	0.56
1913–1950	3.3	−0.7	5.1	1.1	1.81	0.87	0.93
1950–2012	1.5	−0.6	5.3	3.2	3.78	2.08	1.67
2012–2050	1.0	0.6	4.3	3.9	3.28	2.53	0.73
2050–2100	2.8	2.8	4.3	4.3	1.53	1.33	0.17

Source: Supplementary Tables S2.2, S2.4 and S10.3 of Piketty (2014), available online at `http://piketty.pse.ens.fr/en/capital21c2`.

differ seriously in periods as close as the 90's.[7] Therefore, in Piketty, one could probably argue that data for 1970 to 2012 is pretty solid and that it is quite acceptable for the eighteenth and nineteenth centuries in France, the U.K. and the U.S. But the inference to the world level that Piketty makes out of such data is likely less acceptable.

Piketty's guess as to the level of the long-run historical rate of return of capital at the world level is precisely that, only an educated guess which has merit but does not have adequate empirical support. Therefore, his argument that r is relatively stable in the very long run is at least susceptible of conceptual discussion. It seems to us that his argument is questionable, because as the wealth forms change, the relationship between r and other variables changes; and therefore there is not a meaningful comparison between diverse cultures in distinct historical periods. In autocratic societies r could be relatively rigid due to the high relative power of the autocracy, in democracies such power subsists but it is reduced; and the markets expansion gives the productive capital a new logic—very different in nature to the old sumptuous palaces or Egyptians pyramids. Productive capital's expansion necessarily relates to the decreasing returns logic and r becomes inversely related to the size of β.

In summary, 75 years of empirical work show that the elasticity between capital and labor is less than 1.25. Rognlie shows that housing explains 80% of the β increase in the period 1970 to 2010. We have shown that if we remove housing and using β at book value, for all the countries there is an inverse relationship between α and β. Piketty's notion that β in developed countries has a historical U-shaped curve is not corroborated by data. Most of the β increase from 1970 to 2010 is related to the housing boom, the increase in land prices and to price effects between β_{mv} and β_{bv}. But these speculative waves and price effects cannot

---

[7]In the period of 1990 to 2000: for the world, Maddison reports 1.6% average annual growth and the World Bank 3.04% (the difference being influenced by their distinct estimates about the growth of China); for the United States the corresponding values are 2.5% and 3.2%, for the United Kingdom 2.5 and 3.2; for Germany 1.75% and 1.4%; they are only similar for France, 2.0% and 2.1% respectively. The World Bank reports gross and net savings rates since 1970, for France and the world only from 1975; but it only reports g, which requires constant PPP international dollars, since 1990. Maddison reports g since 1970, and even since the year one, but he does not have estimates of the gross and net savings rates.

be a solid base for a long-run forecast. Markets will tend to homogenize the rates of return amongst diverse wealth sectors; therefore the logic of the forecasted relationship between α and β has to be rooted in the productive characteristics of capital. The forecasts have to be in accordance with the empirical findings as to the value of σ.

What will happen in the real world? It is impossible to forecast it, reality can always be subject to speculative movements and short-term price effects. And what will actually happen depends critically in the institutional policies that will be adopted. But from the point of view of theoretical forecasting between two stationary states, we have to be based in the underlying productive forces, leaving aside short to medium term movements which cannot be forecasted. In the long run the law of decreasing returns must operate, as the markets homogenize the r along segments, in all the wealth; therefore, as β increases substantially there is a higher proportional fall in r, and there must be an inverse relationship between α and β.

Finally, let us focus on what could be an alternative scenario for r, assuming Piketty's substantial increase in β, r should be substantially lower, in the range between 1.55% and 2.42%—these estimates are based upon $\sigma = 0.857$, and $\sigma = 1.25$. And now let us imagine that taxes remain at 30%. Then r after taxes could be as low as 1.09% to 1.69%, and $r - g$ could be negative or very small.

The range of r before taxes of 1.55% to 2.42% seems very low compared to its historical values. This is due to the fact that Piketty forecasts a substantial increase in β, of 52%, and the abundance of capital awakens strong decreasing returns which in turn lower r significantly. How much can we trust Piketty's forecast that there will be a substantial increase in β? To answer this question appropriately we will need to go into the next section, where we will explore the relationship between the net savings rate and the real rate of growth of the economy, the determinants of the level of β.

Chapter 3

The dynamics of s

As we have mentioned, the relative rigidity of the net savings rate is also fundamental in Piketty's proposal of capitalism dynamics. Piketty and Zucman (2014, pp. 15–16) argue that their theory is valid for diverse economic growth models, including the dynastic, in which s is a positive function of g. They point out that as long as s moves less than g, β remains a positive function of g. Moreover, they say that there does not seem to be a relationship between s and g, during 1970-2010, when comparing across developed economies (see Table 2.1). These two arguments have been questioned by Krusell and Smith (2015).

The apparent inexistent s and g relation, they argue, is due to institutional differences between the countries. Using postwar U.S. data they show that there is a positive relationship between s and g and that it is strong enough so that as g goes down only small increases in β are obtained. Their results contradict Piketty's forecast that β will substantially increase in the twenty-first century. They also show that Piketty's economic growth model shows key differences with Solow's textbook model as well as with models of endogenous saving optimization.[8]

---

[8]Krusell and Smith, using a constant net savings rate to describe Piketty's model and a production function with labor augmented technology, show that the following relations are different in Piketty's stationary state versus the traditional Solow model in textbooks. Gross and net variables are denoted with subindices b and n, respectively. I) Gross consumption/gross income, $\frac{C_b}{Y_b}$, in Solow is $1 - s_b$, in Piketty is $\frac{(1-s_n)g}{(g+s_n\delta)}$ (where g is the real rate of growth of the economy and δ is the capital depreciation rate). Therefore, in Piketty a lower g is associated with a lower gross consumption/gross income ratio. II) In Piketty the relation between s_b and s_n is given by $s_b = \frac{s_n(g+\delta)}{g+s_n\delta}$, therefore with s_n fixed, s_b goes up aggressively when g falls. In the traditional model, s_n and s_b are related by the equation $s_n = \frac{gs_b}{g+\delta(1-s_b)}$; therefore, with s_b given from outside and constant, when g falls, s_n also falls, and when g goes to zero s_n also goes to zero. Thus, except for the non-interesting case of $s_b = 1$, s_n is a positive function of g. III) $\frac{K}{Y_b}$ in Solow's model is $\frac{s_b}{(g+\delta)}$, and in Piketty's is $\frac{s_n}{(g+s_n\delta)}$; $\frac{K}{Y_n} = \frac{s_n}{g}$ in Piketty (his second fundamental law) and in Solow $\frac{K}{Y_n} = \frac{s_b}{g+\delta(1-s_b)}$.

The consequences are: a) In Piketty with s_n constant, when g goes to zero C_b/Y_b in Piketty goes to zero; therefore s_b goes to 1; b) $\frac{K}{Y_n} = \frac{s_n}{g}$ in Piketty goes to infinity as g goes to zero. While in the traditional model $\frac{K}{Y_n} = \frac{s_b}{g+\delta(1-s_b)}$, therefore, when g goes to zero $\frac{K}{Y_n}$ has a limit $\frac{s_b}{\delta(1-s_b)}$; this limit, using standard values for the world economy of $s_b = 0.2298$ and $\delta = 0.0367$—average values from 1990 to 2010—will be 8.12. (c) $\frac{K}{Y_b}$ has a limit in both cases; in the traditional model the limit will be $\frac{s_b}{\delta} = 6.26$; and in Piketty $\frac{1}{\delta} = 27.23$. d) In the traditional model, changes in s_b take the economy to a new higher growth path and to an increase in K. K in the traditional model, however, cannot grow without bound, because its growth is finally conditioned by

3.1 Solow vs. Piketty. Conceptual differences

In Solow's textbook model the net savings rate is given by the equation $s_n = \frac{gs_b}{g+\delta(1-s_b)}$, and $\frac{K}{Y_n}$ by the expression $\frac{K}{Y_n} = \frac{s_b}{g+\delta(1-s_b)}$. Where s_b is the gross savings rate and δ is the capital depreciation rate. Manipulating the previous expressions one easily obtains $\frac{K}{Y_n} = \frac{s_n}{g}$, Piketty's second fundamental law. However, despite its mathematical identity, conceptual differences remain. In Solow s_b is exogenously given while in Pikkety s_n is assumed relatively rigid. In Solow s_n is a positive function of g. In Solow when g goes to zero there is a limit for $\frac{K}{Y_n}$ given by $\frac{s_b}{\delta(1-s_b)}$. In Piketty with s_n relatively rigid when g goes to zero mathematically $\frac{K}{Y_n}$ goes to infinity – the argument Krusell and Smith have been insisting on; in fact, in economic terms $\frac{K}{Y_n}$ will be restricted in a pikettian economy by the fact that α cannot be greater than one, but anyway it is an unreasonable result. While in Solow s_b is given from outside; in Piketty, with s_n relatively rigid, s_b increases unbounded, since in Piketty's model $s_b = \frac{s_n(g+\delta)}{g+s_n\delta}$.

Using the average historical values for the world economy from 1990 to 2010, $s_b = 22.979\%$ and the estimated capital depreciation rate $\delta = 0.0367$, Table 3.1, compares at several values for g, Solows equation, $\frac{K}{Y_n} = \frac{s_b}{g+\delta(1-s_b)}$, with Piketty's second fundamental law, assuming for Piketty a fixed $s_n = 10\%$. As it can be seen as g becomes very low K/Y_n in Solow tends to its limit, at the values used, of 8.12; while in Piketty it grows unbounded—the point made by Krusell and Smith. In addition as g goes to zero s_n goes to zero in Solows model. But s_b in Piketty's increases unbounded; which is particularly problematic, because at $g = 1.5\%$, the value of his forecast, s_b would be equal to 27.70%, but this value is too high for any historical period of the world economy; data is available since 1975, and at no single year it has been higher than 25, and the average 1975–2012 was 23.14. Thus, it clearly shows that the $s_n = 10\%$ of Piketty is too high. Also in Piketty β is more sensitive to g movements, so when g halves from 3% to 1.5%, β in Piketty doubles, while in Solow it only increases 34.8%. Finally, Solow's β forecast at $g = 1.5\%$ is significantly lower than Pikkety's. Notice that s_n in Solow is a positive function of g, therefore as g goes down to 1.5% s_n goes also down to 7.96%, that is why Solow's forecast is lower than Piketty's.

Solow's model in Table 3.1 is an improvement in Piketty's, because s_n becomes a function of g. However, it must be noticed that since s_b is given from outside, s_b is not a function of g.

---

the law of diminishing returns which says that as capital goes to infinity its marginal product goes to zero— what is known as the Inada condition. In Piketty instead, the change in the net product can be expressed as $F(K, \cdot) - \delta K$, and while $F(K, \cdot) - \delta K$ also satisfies the Inada condition, $F(K, \cdot)$ does not; that is why $\frac{K}{Y_n}$ goes to infinity as g goes to zero. The clue is that while in the traditional model the decreasing return falls below the depreciation rate and stops the growth of capital; in Piketty with an almost fixed high return, capital returns are always high enough for capital to grow unbounded towards the infinity. In economic terms the β growth will be restricted to the value at which capitalists own 100% of income, but it is anyhow a very unsatisfactory result. It is worth pointing out that Krusell and Smith, in their article, use a very high and unsustainable capital depreciation rate of 8%.

Table 3.1: Solow vs. Piketty

g (%)	Solow ($s_b = 22.98\%$, $\delta = 0.0367$)		Piketty ($s_n = 10\%$)	
	β	s_n (%)	β	s_b(%)
3.3	3.75	12.37	3.03	19.01
3.0	3.94	11.83	3.33	19.82
2.1	4.66	9.79	4.76	23.40
1.5	5.31	7.96	6.67	27.70
0.001	8.09	0.08	1000	97.62

Source: The World Bank collection of world development indicators (WDI), July 2014. g is the net national income growth rate at PPP constant international dollars. S_b = gross savings. $s_b = \frac{S_b}{\text{GNI}}$. $S_n = S_b - \delta K$. $s_n = \frac{S_n}{\text{GNI}}$, as reported by the World Bank and then we have $\frac{\delta K}{\text{GNI}} = s_b - s_n$; but s_n in this table is defined according to Piketty's definition $s_n = \frac{S_n}{(\text{GNI} - \delta K)} = \frac{S_n}{\text{GNI}} \cdot \frac{1}{1 - \frac{\delta K}{\text{GNI}}}$. Here $\left(\frac{\delta K}{K}\right) = \delta = \frac{\frac{1}{\beta}\left(\frac{\delta K}{\text{GNI}}\right)}{\left(1 - \frac{\delta K}{\text{GNI}}\right)}$.

3.2 What happens when economic agents optimize?

Krusell and Smith have argued that a dynasties general equilibrium intertemporal optimizing model is incompatible with Piketty, because any rule of intertemporal utility maximization will show that s_n tends to zero as g goes to zero. With $g = 0$, constant capital is expected, therefore s_n must also be equal to zero. Notice that in Solow in Table 3.1 this condition holds.

In a dynastic model (Cass–Koopmans) agents optimize intertemporally and both s_b and s_n become a positive function of g; s_n is more sensitive to g than in a Solow's model because s_b also moves. Krusell and Smith show in postwar U.S. data that both s_b and s_n have decreased as g has gone down. They argue that s_n in the U.S. is actually close to zero today; in 2012 it was 2.63%. What happens at the world level?

We do not have enough historical data to calibrate a dynasties general equilibrium intertemporal optimizing model at the world level; and besides, these models can always be criticized on the grounds that economic agents do not live forever. But since they seem to work well with U.S. data, s_b goes down together with g in the U.S.. It is required to open the question of whether or not s_b is a function of g at the world level. Let us look at some data. Table 3.2 presents results for the periods 1991–2000 and 2001–2012; on which data of s_b, s_n and g are from the World Bank and therefore compatible at the world level. As it can be appreciated, in all countries, except Germany due to the reconstruction of East Germany (see Tables 2.3 and 2.4, where it can be appreciated that β_h explains more than 100% of β despite the fact that housing is undervalued), as well as for the whole world, both s_b and s_n fall as g goes down, and they go up as g increases. This positive relationship could be seen as a confirmation of Krusell and Smith's argument that the model that better suits reality is the dynasties general equilibrium intertemporal optimizing model; but whether this is the case or not, what cannot be denied is that there seems to be, in the real world, a positive relationship between both s_b and s_n, and g.

Table 3.2: g, s_b and s_n

Country	1991–2000			2001–2012		
	$g(\%)$	$s_b(\%)$	$s_n(\%)$	$g(\%)$	$s_b(\%)$	$s_n(\%)$
World	3.01	22.73	10.92	3.64	23.42	11.88
U.S.	3.77	19.24	9.25	1.60	17.22	5.41
U.K.	3.26	15.60	3.92	1.29	14.15	3.32
France	2.16	19.44	8.54	0.96	18.99	7.13
Germany	1.57	20.86	7.44	1.43	22.68	9.31
Japan	0.77	30.18	14.36	0.74	24.38	4.97

Source: World Bank collection of world development indicators (WDI), July 2014.

3.3 Is Piketty's $s_n = 10\%$ too high or not?

From 1975 to 2012 the average world $s_n = 11.93\%$, which at first sight seems to confirm Piketty's 10% assumption. However, during this period the world grew annually an average of 3.34%, versus the 1.5% that Piketty forecasted.[9] Since, as we discuss with detail in the next section, Piketty's forecast consists in making the world converge to the rate of growth of the developed countries, it is then logical to assume that the global savings rate should also converge to the one of these countries.

As it can be seen in Table 3.2 most of the developed countries reduced their growth rate in 2001–2012. In fact as it can be appreciated in Table 3.3 the average rate of growth of four of the most relevant developed countries was only 1.5% in 2001–2010. This period then gives us a good opportunity to analyze how s_b and s_n behave as g falls.[10] There are several methods that can be applied to understand the impact of g in both s_b and s_n. The most straightforward one is to take the weighted s_n average—weighting each country s_n by its respective participation in the GNI sum of all of them in 2010—and use Piketty's model to obtain, at the average historical g of 1.5%, both s_b and β, the answer would be $s_b = 17.76\%$ and $\beta = 4.21$. A more elaborated method would be to take the weighted average of s_b and δ for the period and use a Solow model, in this case one would obtain values, again at the historical average value of $g = 1.5\%$, of $s_n = 6.69\%$ and $\beta = 4.47$ that get closer to the 2001–2010 historical average values of $s_n = 6.30\%$ and $\beta = 4.44$. An even more sophisticated method would be to use a Solow model for each country, letting s_b and δ fixed at their country average historical 2001–2010 values and finding out the country β and s_n in each case. Once we have an estimated s_n for each country, we obtain their weighted average value; and using $g = 1.5\%$ we obtain β. This third method gives us $s_n = 6.40\%$ and $\beta = 4.27$. As the reader can appreciate the three methods provide similar results. Table 3.3 presents the results using the third method.

---

[9]These two numbers are not fully compatible, the 3.34% refers to GNI while the 1.5% refers to net GNI. We did not obtain the growth of net GNI because Maddison 1975 to 1990 is not compatible with The World Bank. But in any case the net GNI growth was clearly above 3%.

[10]If one looked at the period 1990–2010 as an stationary state, it would seem to be better defined by Solow's model than by Pikkety's. The averages in the period were as follows: $s_b = 22.98\%$, $s_n = 11.32\%$, $\delta = 0.0367$, $\beta = 4.12$, and $g = 3.68\%$. With Pikety, using the average s_n of the period, one obtains $\beta = 3.07$ and $s_b = 20.31\%$. With Solow $\beta = 3.53$ and $s_n = 13\%$.

Table 3.3: Using Solow's model to estimate the s_n of the 21st century

| Country | 2001–2010 | | | | $g = 1.5\%$ | $g = 2.1\%$ |
	g (%)	β	s_n (%)	s_b (%)	s_n (%)	s_n (%)
U.S.	1.60	4.43	5.83	17.60	6.61	8.02
U.K.	1.68	4.96	4.02	14.56	6.43	7.38
France	0.95	4.94	7.63	19.29	5.54	9.18
Germany	1.28	3.82	9.06	22.47	6.02	7.96
Weighted Average	1.4959	4.44	6.30	18.18	6.40	8.07
β estimate	–	–	–	–	4.27	3.84

Sources: s_b and s_n from Table 2.8. In the last two columns s_n is estimated with a Solow's model. We take the historical average value for s_b, introduce it into the model and, using the methodology of Table 3.1, we obtain for each country the corresponding s_n. Then we obtain the weighted average again with the 2010 participation of each country in the sum of the GNI of all.

In Table 3.3 we also calculate the s_n and β that would correspond to a $g = 2.1\%$; which is related to the scenario that we will be presenting in the next section. To find these values we assume that s_b is directly proportional to g. So that if g falls/rises, s_b also falls/rises in the same proportion that g moved in each one of the four developed countries in the table, between the periods 1991–2000 vs. 2001–2010.

The results in Table 3.3 are interesting. At $g = 1.5\%$ the average s_n is 6.40% and the countries range is 5.54% to 6.61%; which again confirms that Piketty's s_n assumption of 10% is too high. At $g = 2.1\%$ the average is 8.07% and the range is 7.38 to 9.18%.

In summary, If s_b and s_n fallen in the world in the second half of the twenty-first century as they did in the four developed countries in Table 3.3, during 2001–2010, the corresponding s_n at $g = 1.5\%$ would be 6.40% and at $g = 2.1\%$ it would be 8.07%.

3.4 Piketty's theoretical difficulties

Piketty's two fundamental laws are essentially an economic theory that tells us that s_n and r are relatively rigid. But the problem with such a theory is that it is not compatible with economic agents' optimizing behaviour in a disaggregate economy. Piketty's proposal to identify capital with wealth creates theoretical confusion. Capital is about quantities, it is related to productivity and production; it is an input in a production function. Wealth can incorporate, in addition to capital, speculative housing behaviour and other price effects. But in the long run as markets equalize the rates of return around markets, the rate of return in total wealth must be governed by the rate of return of capital. Moreover the savings rate must be a function of g, because if it is not, it actually implies changes in the productivity of capital that cannot be understood. To clarify this point we will look at some examples.

First if we look at Table 2.8 we notice that in the first millennia $g = 0$ and $r = 4.5\%$, and this is not well explained by Piketty; but in order for β not to go to infinity g cannot be zero it has to be a very small number say $g = 0.000001$, and s_n has to be also very small to get a meaningful β value. Let us say that we want a β of 7 then $s_n = 0.000007$; and with $r = 4.5\%$, $\alpha = 31.5\%$. So far so good, historically a very low s_n makes sense. But then the theoretical question comes: s_n has to be very low when g is very low or the model does not make sense, but then this implies that s_n must move with g.

We need a theory that links s_n with g, and just arguing that s_n is relatively rigid is not good enough. In Solow's model, s_b is given from outside and the model explains that a higher s_b is related to a higher growth path, one associated with a higher initial income per capita. Once we are in the growth path any income per-capita growth is compatible with any s_n, but initially the whole purpose of increasing s_b was to move to a higher growth path. Saving must have a productive purpose. One cannot just move s_n without understanding what is the economic theoretical productive story that is related to such an increase. The following example will bring this point forward.

Let us imagine two stationary states X and Z. Let us assume that population does not grow in neither of them, that we have full employment and that the labor force that we denote by LF, to distinguish it from labor income L, does not grow either and it is the same in both economies. Let us make income the numeraire, $Y = 1$. The stationary state X reproduces Piketty's forecast for the second half of the twenty-first century with $s_n = 10\%$, $r = 4.3\%$ and $g = 1.5\%$; therefore $\beta = 6.7$ and $\alpha = 28.7\%$. The stationary state Z will be defined as a function of the long-term interest of the capitalists. Since the capitalists have control upon the net savings rate, s_n, the question is, What happens if they raise it from 10% to 20%? The answer in a Pikettian economy is that $\beta = 13.33$, and $\alpha = 0.573$. Since $Y = 1$, then $C = \alpha$. The capitalists will optimize then the present discounted value of their income, which we will denote by C_{pv}. In general terms $C_{pv} = \frac{\alpha}{r-g}$; the value of an infinite series with an initial value α which grows at g and is discounted at r. Then for the stationary state X; $C_{pv} = \frac{0.287}{0.043-0.015} = 10.25$. And for the stationary state Z; $C_{pv} = \frac{0.573}{0.043-0.015} = 20.46$. It means that the capitalists not only increase their share in total income but also the present discounted value of their income. Since s_n is to be decided by the capitalists then they should increase it until they obtain the maximum possible income. Note that $\alpha = \frac{rs_n}{0.015}$, therefore if $\alpha = 1$, then $s_n = \frac{0.015}{0.043} = 0.349$; which means that if the capitalist save 34.9%, they will own 100% of the national income.

In fact they will be restricted by the minimum subsistence salary that they would need to give to the labor force. Let w equal the subsistence salary, then $w \cdot LF = L$, the labor income. And the share of labor in income will be $L/Y = L$. α then will be $1 - L$. The s_n which optimizes C_{pv} is the one that gives as a solution $\alpha = 1 - L$. Since C_{pv} is an increasing monotonic function of s_n (because $C_{pv} = s \times 102.38$), C_{pv} always grows as s_n grows. Thus, to maximize C_{pv}, s_n will grow until $\alpha = 1 - L$. But since LF does not grow and P, the population, neither, then $g = G/P = G$, where G is the product growth in real terms. Since w is a subsistence salary expressed in real terms it does not grow either, therefore $w \cdot LF$ does not grow. Thus, as time t goes to infinity, $\frac{w \cdot LF}{Y}$ goes to zero and $\alpha = 1 - w \cdot LF$ goes to 1; therefore s_n goes to the limit of 34.9% and C_{pv} goes to 35.7%.

In summary, the problem with Piketty's economic dynamics is that it would imply that in the long run, if the capitalists maximize their interest, they will have all the income of the economy. A result which is not very interesting and clearly difficult to defend.

Of course it could be argued against the previous intellectual exercise that the capitalists do not calculate their interest in the infinite horizon. But the point of the exercise is not to argue that they do, the purpose is to expose the theoretical problems of Piketty's proposal. In

Piketty's proposal economic agents do not optimize, in fact if they do his theoretical model is unsustainable. It is not possible to develop a theoretical model of income distribution as Piketty pretends without having both r and s linked theoretically to the production process of the economy. The reason, in the real world, why capitalist do not increase their saving so much is because they face decreasing returns. In Piketty, with r relatively rigid the capitalists can increase s and always increase their income share; in a productive economy they cannot because of diminishing returns.

3.5 What is the problem? Another example to further understand what is happening

Let us imagine again an economy with zero population growth and that LF is constant and it is the numeraire, then $LF = 1$. And let us assume that the initial product per capita is 2, thus the product $Y = 2$. If $g = 0.01$ and $s_n = 0.05$, then $\beta = 5$ and $K = 10$. The production technique in such economy is $10K$ and $1L$ produce $2Y$. In the second period the production technique will be $10.1K$ and $1L$ producing $2.02Y$ and so on. What happens if g falls to $g = 0.001$? Then $\beta = 50$ and $K = 100$. The production technique is now such that $100K$ and $1L$ produce $2Y$. And in the second period $100.1K$ and $1L$ produce $2.002Y$, and so on. What happened that the economy needs much more capital to produce the same product? K/Y increasing means that capital productivity is going down, and then there is the need to have a productive story of why this happens: Piketty does not have it. K/Y movements do not only relate to an income distribution story, they also are necessarily related to a story of the productivity of capital—a story that Piketty never develops.

It is true that once in a growth path, two stationary states can have the same g and different s_n, but the level of such growth paths is given by the difference in the initial push of the difference in savings rates. In addition if K goes up, as we saw in the previous section r must go down.

The relative rigidity in r and s_n that Piketty introduces causes all kind of theoretical nonsense stories, we already saw that as g goes to zero β goes to infinity and s_b grows unbounded, but also notice that as β grows a lot, for example if it reaches 50, α would be equal to 215%. Thus or β grows less or r falls or both things happen.

That g falls does not necessarily must imply that K/Y must go up. If s_n falls proportionally to g, then s_n would be equal to 0.005, and β would be again equal to 5 and $K = 10$. The technique of production then is not modified, and the productivity of capital remains the same.

From a productive point of view, the only reason for capital to go up to 100 would have to be that it is associated with a considerable increase in initial Y, so that initial Y/L, the level of the growth path, is substantially higher. The K level is not linked to g, but it has to be to the initial per capita product. How much would initial Y have to go up in the previous example? To solve this, suppose the terminal r used by Piketty of 0.043. When $g = 0.01$ we can observe that the product present discounted value, Y_{pv}, is $\left(\frac{2}{0.043-0.01}\right) = 60.606$, and capital present discounted value, K_{pv}, is $\left(\frac{10}{0.043-0.01}\right) = 303.03$. There are no surprises and K/Y is then 5.

What we want to find is the value of initial Y such that when $g = 0.001$, K/Y stays in 5. In order to do that, observe that K_{pv} is now $\left(\frac{100}{0.043-0.01}\right) = 2380.95$. Therefore Y_{pv} would have to be equal to 476.19 for K/Y to remain in 5. Now if Y_{pv} is 476.19, then no surprises, the initial Y has to be 20—this result is of course general at any level of r.

Then as g falls from 0.01 to 0.001 one of three things needs to happen, or a combination of them: 1) s falls proportionally to g and K/Y remains unchanged, 2) K goes up and the economy moves into a new growth path in which initial Y also goes up and therefore K/Y remains unchanged (notice in here that g may be the same as before but it starts from an initial higher Y), 3) K/Y goes up. But in this third alternative it is necessary to explain why the productivity of capital goes down. 1) is not compatible with Piketty's assumption of a relatively rigid s_n; 2) is not compatible with Piketty because he assumes that the growth rate of the developed countries goes down starting 2012. And there is never a discussion as to the transitional consequences on economic growth related to the increase in β. Therefore, in Piketty, initial Y never goes up. Then, 3) is Piketty's selected option. But then an explanation is needed of why the productivity of capital is going down, particularly with the increase in β of 50% forecasted by this author, but he never provides such explanation.

For β to go up 50% one of two explanations has to be provided: 1) the productivity of capital goes down dramatically, or 2) the increase is explained by speculative housing waves and/or price effects. But 2), as we have been arguing is only valid in the short to medium term, moreover Piketty does not have an explanation of this type either. And 1) is just not believable, because there is no reason for capital to become so unproductive. Moreover, if it did then the rate of return on capital, r, should also go down dramatically—and as we saw in the previous section, a higher β leads to a higher proportional fall in r.

It must be noticed that the direct relationship between s_b and s_n with g should not necessarily hold for any period and for any country, if a country chooses to increase his savings rate in order to foster a higher future transitional growth for a given period, s_b and s_n may increase with g going down, so the relationship can be inverse temporarily as it happens with Germany in Table 3.2. The high s_n in Germany as we said is due to the reconstruction of East Germany. But when comparing stationary states in which s_n remains fixed at the level required in each stationary state, the relationship must be necessarily direct, unless a higher s_n can be related to a previous higher transitional growth, which is not the case with Piketty's forecast.

Also it must be pointed out that while it is true that the long-run growth in western capitalism cannot be explained only for higher savings rates, and therefore the expansion of knowledge must be introduced (and it explains most of the growth); that does not mean that any level of s_n can go with any level of g. The purpose of saving is always a higher transitional growth. Besides, for some countries higher savings were absolutely crucial in their development, the Asian miracle cannot be explained without high savings.

For Piketty there can be different stationary states with similar saving levels but diverse g's, which will then be traduced into also different β's. In what follows we will quote a long paragraph from Piketty because it is crucial to understand his logic: "In other words, for a savings rate on the order of 10–12 percent and a growth rate of national income per capita on the order of 1.5–2 percent a year, it follows immediately that a country that has near zero demographic growth and therefore a total growth rate in the order 1.5–2 percent, as in Europe, can expect to accumulate a capital stock worth six to eight years of national income, whereas a country with demographic growth in the order of I percent a year and therefore a total growth rate of 2.5–3 percent, as in the United States, will accumulate a capital stock worth only three to four years of national income. And if the latter country tends to save a little less than the former, perhaps because its population is not aging as rapidly, this mechanism will be further reinforced as a result. In other words, countries with similar growth rates of income per capita can end up with very different capital/income ratios simply because their demographic growth rates are not the same. This allows us to give good account of the historical evolution of the capital/income ratio." Piketty (2014, p. 167).

How should we read the previous paragraph? Given the savings rate, everything he affirms is correct. But the problem is that s_n is a function of g, therefore it does not make sense to maintain it fixed, or almost fixed, as one makes the comparison that he does. To further enhance our argument we will introduce another example.

Let us imagine an economy where everybody works and initially $LF = 1$, but it grows at 0.02, $g = 0.01$, $s_n = 0.05$ and $Y/L = 2$. Then, again $\beta = 5$ and $K = 10$. But g can be decomposed in 0.5 productivity and 0.02 population growth. The production technique will be $10K$ and $1L$ produce $2Y$ and in the second period $10.1K$ and $1.02L$ produce $2.02Y$, and so on. If we reduce the demographic growth rate to 0.01, g will be equal to 0.005; and if we maintain $s = 0.05$, then $\beta = 10$ and $K = 20$. Piketty's forecast holds, β grows and the income distribution deteriorates because the fall in the demographic growth. But notice what happened, the new technique of production is $20K$ and $1L$ produce $2Y$ and in the second period $20.1K$ and $1.01L$ produce $2.01Y$, and so on. Therefore, capital is only half as productive as before. If we want to maintain the same capital productivity as previously, which means a constant K/Y, then the savings rate must go down proportionally to g. If the savings rate goes down to 0.025, then technology will remain the same, $\beta = 5$ and $K = 10$; and the production technique in the first and subsequent periods does not change. In the first period $10K$ and $1L$ produce $2Y$ and in the second period $10.05K$ and $1.01L$ produce $2.01Y$, and so on. Note that 10.05 : 2.01 :: 10.1 : 2.02. Observe, that if there is less demographic growth, for the productivity of capital to remain the same, s_n has to go down proportionally to g, and then β remains the same. If β changes it has to be related to productivity story or to an initial change in the output per worker which would mean a higher transitory growth. Since Piketty does not contemplate a higher transitory growth, then his β increase has to be related to less productive capital. But then he does not have an answer for why capital is less productive. And also, as we mentioned, if for any reason capital became less productive, then one couldn't assume a rigid r as he does.

What deteriorates the income distribution in Piketty's example is not the fall in the rate of demographic growth, but the fact that he maintains s_n rigid, or almost rigid. And this s_n rigidity, as g falls, is necessarily linked to less productive capital and he never discusses or explains what the source of the reduced productivity is.

Maybe the most important figure in Piketty (2014) is 5.8, which shows the historical tendency of β and its forecast at the world level. The forecast in Figure 5.8 is a simulation that goes from the actual β value in 2010, 440, to the value forecasted for 2100, 667. Table

Table 3.4: Piketty's world β forecast

Year	β (%) Simulated	β (%) Geom. Growth	Period	s	Period	g (%)
2010	440	440	2010–2020	0.172		
					2012–2030	3.4
2020	450	461	2020–2030	0.169		
2030	502	483	2030–2040	0.187	2030–2050	3.1
2040	513	505				
2050	557	529	2040–2050	0.182		
2060	605	554	2050–2060	0.157	2050–2070	1.7
2070	614	581	2060–2070	0.106		
2080	627	608	2070–2080	0.106	2070–2100	1.4
2090	643	637	2080–2090	0.100	2012–2050	3.3
2100	667	667	2090–2100	0.100	2050–2100	1.5

Source: Supplemental Tables S2.2, S2.3, S10.3, S12.4a and S12.4b of Piketty (2014), available at http://piketty.pse.ens.fr/en/capital21c2.

3.4 presents the data related to figure 5.8.

In a basic sense the entire simulated forecast is defined by the terminal stationary state of $s_n = 10\%$ and $g = 1.5\%$, which gives a $\beta = 6.67$ in the year 2100. In the second column we have introduced a simple geometric growth adjustment from the 2010 actual value of 440% to the terminal value of 667%, observe that it is almost identical to Piketty's simulation. Why is this relevant? Because it shows that the whole forecast crucially depends on the terminal stationary state. But since s_n is a function of g, as we have shown, then Piketty's terminal stationary state is inadequate (because he did assume a too high s_n); and then the whole simulation in Table 3.4 has to be questioned.

In summary, Piketty's two fundamental laws are an economic theory that argues for the relative rigidity of r and s_n, but they do not make theoretical sense. Piketty is wrong and that is why the title of this essay. He has confused historical statistics that include speculative housing movements and other price effects with what happens to capital; and for a long-run forecast, as markets equalize the rates of return across them, only the dynamics of capital is relevant. Moreover, his rigidity in s_n has the consequence that his forecast of $s_n = 10\%$ is too high. In the conclusion we present scenarios with more adequate (lower) s_n values compatible with Table 3.3.

Chapter 4

The dynamics of g

Piketty argues that economic growth in the twenty-first century will decelerate because growth in the twentieth century was due to two specific temporary phenomena: 1) The two wars reconstruction, and 2) The developing countries convergence. The first will not repeat itself, and the second will continue in the twenty-first century, but only in the first half because such convergence will happen rapidly. Therefore, the world will enter in the second half of the twenty-first century in what he has called the end of growth. For Piketty long-term growth is explained by the diffusion of knowledge, a public good, and the convergence between countries is due to the diffusion of such knowledge. For the second half of the twenty-first century he forecasts lower growth based on three assumptions: 1) a fall in the population growth rate; 2) a fall in the per capita income growth in developed countries; 3) the convergence of developing countries with developed ones will occur in the first half of the twenty-first century; therefore there is a positive effect in the rate of growth of the world economy in the first half that will dissipate in the second half.

The fall in the global population growth rate closely follows the United Nations forecast and it seems acceptable to us. But the other two assumptions are questionable.

The argument of the transitory effect of the two wars in the GDP per capita growth rate of developed countries seems unsustainable. The developed world growth rate from 1970–2012 was similar to 1913–2012 and was around 1.8%, much higher than Piketty's 1.2% (see Table 4.2); and by 1970 the wars reconstruction effects were mostly over. Therefore, without the wars argument, the only remaining explanation for the drastic fall in g is the deceleration of technology, which is highly unlikely.

As to the argument of the rapid convergence of the developing countries, it also seems inadequate. If the convergence occurred, it would have to be slower than what he forecasts. Therefore, the convergence process will continue in the second half of the twenty-first century. Thus, it is highly unlikely that the world economic growth rate will substantially fall in the second half in relation to the first half as he proposes. In fact, if Piketty's forecast materialized, it would mean, as we will show, the end of poverty and of the highly unequal income distribution among countries; we identify both outcomes as low probability events.

In what follows we will review the historical economic growth data for developed and developing economies and we will build an alternative scenario. The purpose is not to argue that our scenario is more likely than Piketty's one, because at almost 100 years away it is impossible to forecast what will really happen. The purpose is to show that Piketty's forecast is not sustainable, based only upon data, and that his theoretical conjectures are highly questionable.

4.1 The deceleration of growth in developed countries

Pikkety proposes that in the rest of the twenty-first century Western Europe, North America, Japan and Australia will grow only 1.2% (see Table 4.1). However these regions and countries grew from 1970–2012 more than 1.8%, almost the same as 1913–2012. They achieved this growth even though the reconstruction was mostly over and despite the 2008 financial crisis (see Table 4.2). Therefore the war reconstruction argument to defend the announced deceleration has little support.

Table 4.1: Economic Growth in the 21st century (GDP per capita growth, Annual %)

Country or Region	Piketty's scenario			Proposed scenario
	2012–2050	2050–2100	2012–2100	2012-2100
World	2.5	1.3	1.85	1.82
Western Europe	1.2	1.2	1.20	1.80
Eastern Europe	2.7	1.2	1.86	1.80
Russia and others	2.7	1.2	1.86	1.80
North America	1.2	1.2	1.20	1.80
Latin America	2.7	1.7	2.15	1.70
Northern Africa	4.5	1.7	2.89	1.80
Sub-Saharan Africa	4.5	1.7	2.89	1.00
China	4.5	1.3	2.67	3.00
India	4.5	1.7	2.89	2.30
Japan	1.2	1.2	1.20	1.80
Australia	1.2	1.2	1.20	1.80
Middle East	2.7	1.7	2.15	1.80
Central Asia	2.7	1.7	2.15	1.00
Other Asian countries	2.7	1.7	2.15	2.50

Source: Author's calculations based on Supplementary Tables TS2.2d and CTS1.3 (Excel version) of Piketty (2014), available at http://piketty.pse.ens.fr/en/capital21c2.
The proposed scenario is a qualitative judgement based on the historical tendencies shown in Table 4.2. We have used 1.8% for the developed world instead of Piketty's 1.2%, considering that Western Europe and North America grew above 1.8% during 1970–2012. We also use this value for Eastern Europe, Russia and others, Northern Africa and the Middle East. For Latin America we use the value of 1.7% observed during 1913–2012 and 1970–2012. Sub-Saharan Africa and Central Asia performed very badly in 1970-2012, therefore we use 1.0% which is closer to their performance in 1913-2012. China, India and other Asian Countries do not show the difference between the first and the second half of the twenty-first century that Piketty proposes. China (3%) and other Asian Countries (2.5%) will grow faster, while India (2.3%) does it slower. This reflects our belief that in the first two cases the development model is more sustainable in the long run. For the World the estimate is based on each region's forecast, taking into account the population and the GDP per capita growth for each region. The population comes from the Supplementary Table TS2.2d.

The growth in the product per capita has to do with technology, which relates to the globalization process, the expansion of the markets, knowledge accumulation and other fac-

Table 4.2: Historical GDP per capita growth rates (Annual %)

Country or Region	1990–2012	1820–1913	1913–1950	1950–2012	1913–2012	1820–2012	1970–2012
World	2.1	0.9	0.9	2.1	1.6	1.3	1.7
Western Europe	1.5	1.1	0.8	2.6	1.9	1.5	1.9
Eastern Europe	3.1	1.0	0.6	2.6	1.9	1.4	2.1
Russia and others	2.1	0.8	1.8	2.3	2.1	1.5	1.8
North America	1.4	1.6	1.6	1.9	1.8	1.7	1.8
Latin America	2.1	0.8	1.4	1.9	1.7	1.3	1.7
Northern Africa	2.2	0.8	0.6	2.2	1.6	1.2	2.1
Sub-Saharan Africa	1.3	0.3	1.0	1.0	1.0	0.7	0.5
China	9.4	−0.1	−0.6	4.2	2.4	1.2	5.7
India	4.7	0.3	−0.2	2.3	1.3	0.8	2.9
Japan	0.7	0.8	0.9	4.0	2.8	1.8	1.9
Australia	2.0	2.6	1.1	2.0	1.6	2.1	1.8
Middle East	2.5	0.6	1.5	2.5	2.1	1.4	1.8
Central Asia	−0.8	0.8	1.8	0.8	1.2	1.0	−0.4
Other Asian countries	3.2	0.4	−0.2	3.2	1.9	1.2	3.5

Source: Supplementary Table CS1.3 of Piketty (2014), available at `http://piketty.pse.ens.fr/en/capital21c2`

tors; and there is no reason to assume that they will not continue growing like in the past, particularly if one is to build a long-term forecast. Once the war argument is discarded, based on the data, a forecasted growth of 1.8% for the developed countries seems more reasonable than Piketty's 1.2%.

Table 4.3 shows the participation of countries and regions in the global product. As it can be appreciated Pikkety's forecast represents a rupture with the historical tendency; according to him the participation of the main developed countries (Western Europe, North America, Japan and Australia) will fall in 2100 to less than a half of the 2010 value. The scenario that we propose, in instead, assumes the historical tendency; thus, it maintains in 2100 today's relative importance of the developed countries.

4.2 The rapid convergence of the developing countries

Piketty's forecast is based upon a rapid convergence due to the deceleration of the developed world and the rapid growth of the developing one. The main convergence will last only 38 years, after which China grows like the developed economies, and the convergence of other countries will decelerate (see Table 4.1). It is due to this rapid convergence that the world economic growth falls in Piketty's model in the second half of the century in relationship to the first half; as it can be seen in Table 4.4, growth falls from 2.5% in 2012–2050, to 1.5% in 2050–2070 and to 1.2% in 2070–2100. Thus, the convergence ends in 2070, after which all the world grows 1.2%, like the developed countries.

Piketty's forecasted fall in the growth rate is easy to understand. The developed countries grow 1.2% all the period. The main convergence happens the first 38 years and that is why growth equals 2.5% during these years. The following 20 years convergence continues but at a lower pace and during this period the world grows still faster than the developed economies. Finally, in 2070 convergence is over, and the last 30 years the entire world grows at the same pace, 1.2% annually.

Table 4.3: Product Distribution (percentage of global product)

Country or Region	2012	Piketty's scenario	Proposed scenario
World	100.0	100.0	100.0
Western Europe	17.8	7.4	12.7
Eastern Europe	2.8	1.5	1.5
Russia and others	4.3	2.3	2.2
North America	20.0	12.0	20.7
Latin America	8.8	9.1	6.4
Northern Africa	1.4	3.0	1.2
Sub-Saharan Africa	2.6	16.5	3.3
China	14.6	14.3	19.6
India	5.7	11.9	7.4
Japan	5.3	1.5	2.6
Australia	1.1	0.7	1.2
Middle East	5.6	9.0	6.8
Central Asia	0.7	0.8	0.3
Other Asian countries	9.1	10.1	14.1
Developed world*	44.3	21.6	37.3
The rest of the world	55.7	78.4	62.7

Source: Author's calculations based on Supplementary Tables S1.1b, S2.2d and CS1.3 (Excel version) of Piketty (2014), from the set of spreadsheet files available at http://piketty.pse.ens.fr/en/capital21c2. The first column is estimated using the 2012 output data from Table SI.1b. The other columns are estimated using the population (Table TS2.2d) and GDP per capita in 2100 to calculate each region's output and its participation to the world output. In Piketty's scenario the GDP per capita is taken from Table CS1.3, while for the proposed scenario it is calculated from the 2012 GDP per capita (Table CS1.3), using the growth rates proposed in Table 4.1.
*Includes Western Europe, North America, Japan and Australia.

Table 4.4: World GDP and population growth rates during 2012–2100

Period	Piketty's Scenario			Proposed Scenario		
	World GDP growth (%)	GDP per capita growth (%)	Population growth (%)	World GDP growth (%)	GDP per capita growth (%)	Population growth (%)
2012–2100	2.28	1.86	0.41	2.32	1.82	0.49
2012–2050	3.28	2.53	0.73	2.63	1.82	0.79
2050–2100	1.53	1.33	0.17	2.08	1.82	0.26
2012–2030	3.54	2.59	0.92	2.82	1.82	0.97
2030–2050	3.05	2.48	0.56	2.46	1.82	0.63
2050–2070	1.74	1.47	0.27	2.19	1.82	0.37
2070–2100	1.39	1.24	0.10	2.00	1.82	0.18

Source: Supplementary Tables S2.2d, S2.4, and CS1.3 of Piketty (2014), available at http://piketty.pse.ens.fr/en/capital21c2. Piketty's population growth rates are slightly different than ours since we have used the latest version (June 2013 version, consulted in May 22, 2015) of the World Population Prospects of the United Nations (see http://esa.un.org/unpd/wpp/index.htm), instead of the one used by Piketty (April 2011). Particularly, this implies a World GDP growth of 2.08% during 2050–2100, instead of the 1.98% that would be obtained using Piketty's population growth rates. This small variation makes no difference from a theoretical perspective.

Table 4.5: Historical convergence vs. Piketty (GDP per capita annual growth rate vs. the average of Western Europe and North America)

Country or Region	1950–2012	1970–2012	2012–2100 Piketty's Scenario	Proposed Scenario
World	0.86	0.94	1.75	1.00
Western Europe	1.16	0.99	1.00	1.00
Eastern Europe	1.20	1.12	1.77	1.00
Russia and others	0.98	0.95	1.77	1.00
North America	0.79	0.96	1.00	1.00
Latin America	0.77	0.93	2.27	0.92
Northern Africa	0.92	1.11	4.29	1.00
Sub-Saharan Africa	0.43	0.56	4.29	0.50
China	3.08	4.81	3.56	2.80
India	0.95	1.55	4.29	1.54
Japan	2.72	1.03	1.00	1.00
Australia	0.81	0.99	1.00	1.00
Middle East	1.14	0.97	2.27	1.00
Central Asia	0.39	0.38	2.27	0.50
Other Asian countries	1.68	1.95	2.27	1.83

Source: Author's calculations based on Supplementary Tables (Excel version) of Piketty (2014), available online at http://piketty.pse.ens.fr/en/capital21c2. For the first two columns we first estimate the weighted average GDP per capita growth rate for Western Europe and North America for each period, taking into account the GDP per capita of each region and its population. Then we divide each region GDP per capita growth rate by the previous average. The population data come from the Supplementary Table S2.2d, and the GDP per capita comes from table CS1.3. For the last two columns the average is straightforward from our Table 4.1, and it is 1.2% for Piketty and 1.8% for the proposed scenario; the regional and world GDP per-capita growth rates for this period also come from our Table 4.1.

But how likely is Piketty's convergence story? Piketty argues that Asia and Africa converged to the developed world rapidly after 1950, see Figure 1.3 in Piketty (2014). Table 4.5 shows the historical convergence versus Piketty's forecast and ours. One is equal to the average growth of Western Europe and North America. A value less than one implies divergence, while a value greater than one signals convergence. As it can be seen, a significant appreciable convergence between 1950 and 2012—the period of Figure 1.3 of Piketty (2014)—only occurs with China, Japan and the Asian countries. During this period China grew 3.08 times the average of Western Europe and North America, Japan 2.72 times and the other Asian countries 1.68 times.

From 1950 to 2012 one can observe, in Table 4.5, the second war reconstruction phenomena; Western Europe grew significantly faster than North America, that is why it grew faster than the average of both; Eastern Europe also grew faster during this period. But note that the reconstruction effect had been finished by 1970; because the 1970–2012 growth in Western Europe and North America is almost the same, and the reconstruction only continues, at a slower pace, in Eastern Europe.

From 1970 to 2012 Japan's convergence is already very minimal, but China and the other Asian countries continue converging; China's convergence is particularly aggressive in this period, growing almost five times the average of Western Europe and North America. In this period also India has a significant convergence and Northern Africa a moderate one.

Piketty's convergence scenario is too aggressive and does not have historical precedents. Sub-Saharan Africa and Northern Africa converge aggressively, growing 4.3 times the average of Western Europe and North America from 2012 to 2100. Sub-Saharan Africa has drastically diverged in the past, it grew the last 62 years less than half the average of Western Europe and North America, and the last 42 years less than 60% of the mentioned average (see Table 4.5). Northern Africa grew the last 62 years 0.92 of the used indicator and the last 42 years it did converge, but only moderately, growing 1.11 times the reference indicator. Central Asia grew in both periods around 0.40 of the previously mentioned indicator, Piketty forecasts that it will grow more than the double, 2.30.

What does this mean? That the poorest region in the planet will converge and they will not be any longer poor. Since all forecasts are made at constant 2012 Euros with similar purchasing power, they are in principle comparable across time and between countries. Compare in Table 4.6 Piketty's 2100 forecast with the 2012 actual levels. As it can be appreciated in Piketty's forecast the poorest regions on earth have a per-capita income that would classify them today as developed. Note also that all the underdeveloped countries and regions converge aggressively towards the developing countries. Piketty's forecast ends up with poverty. But to achieve this, he assumes growth rates in the developing countries which are almost impossible to be realized. Sub-Saharan Africa would need to have a sustained real growth of 2.89% for 88 years, which implies growing 4.5% in real terms for 38 years (see Table 4.1). But no country or region had similar achievement. In the twentieth century, from 1913 to 2012, the highest growth rate belongs to Japan and it is only of 2.8%; and from 1950 to 2012 the highest belongs to China and it is of 4.2% (see Table 4.2). Not only Sub-Saharan Africa would need to break all the historical records in the next 38 years, but also Northern Africa, China and India, see Table 4.1. Moreover all the other regions and countries, with the exception of the developed ones, would have to grow 2.7% in real terms the next 38 years. Again observe in Table 4.2 that for prolonged periods only China, Japan and the other Asian countries were able to outperform such a growth rate.

Piketty's forecast implies that growth in all the underdeveloped countries must be the same or better than the historical record of the Asian miracle. This forecast, in our opinion, implies a misunderstanding of the Asian economic model. This model has a driving technological motor, its exports to developed countries—where the changing preferences of a broad middle class give direction to the technological progress. But the developed economies have a limited import capacity, which necessarily restricts the technological speed of convergence of the rest of the world. This is particularly true in Piketty's forecast, where the participation of the developed economies in the global product goes to a half of its actual value.

The critical point to understand is that the convergence of the Asian miracle was due to specific economic policies. And even though the convergence has its own logic, because as manual labor becomes expensive, countries with fast development look for other countries with cheaper manual labor, it is very difficult to forecast the future magnitude of such phenomena as well as to precise the speed and time in which it will happen.

The convergence is based in an exporting model that requires that developed economies do import, and even though there is no reason to believe that this tendency will change, one should not forget the economic damage suffered by Japan as a consequence of changing

Table 4.6: GDP per capita in Piketty's scenario: 2012 vs. 2100 (PPP, 2012 Euros)

Country or Region	2012	% of the weighted average of Western Europe and North America	2100	% of the weighted average of Western Europe and North America
World	10 092	28.6	50 485	48.8
Western Europe	30 689	87.0	87 675	84.8
Eastern Europe	15 976	45.3	80 919	78.3
Russia and others	15 363	43.6	77 814	75.3
North America	40 664	115.3	116 170	112.4
Latin America	10 435	29.6	67 612	65.4
Northern Africa	5741	16.3	70 310	68.0
Sub-Saharan Africa	2045	5.8	25 050	24.2
China	7673	21.8	77 940	75.4
India	3200	9.1	39 194	37.9
Japan	29 999	85.1	85 701	82.9
Australia	29 486	83.6	84 238	81.5
Middle East	13 390	38.0	86 762	83.9
Central Asia	6375	18.1	41 309	40.0
Other Asian countries	5665	16.1	36 705	35.5

Sources: Author's calculations based on Supplementary Tables (Excel version) of Piketty (2014), available online at `http://piketty.pse.ens.fr/en/capital21c2`. Here we first estimate the weighted average GDP per capita for Western Europe and North America for 2012 and 2100, taking into account their relative populations. Then we divide the GDP per capita of each region by this average. The required populations come from the Supplementary Table TS2.2d and the GDP per capita from Table CTS1.3

commercial policies implemented by the Clinton administration.

There is no basis to argue that the future will be significantly different than the past. China and India have enormous populations, which mostly have not yet converged, and the rest of the underdeveloped world has much to do to be able to converge. Based upon historical evidence the convergence will be a long and partial process that will positively impact the growth of the world economy for a very long time, and which will maintain the underdeveloped world still far away, as to product per capita is concerned, from the developed countries. To change this scenario it is required that the developed world adopts specific policies to promote the underdeveloped world growth – something like the Marshall Plan, those policies today do not seem highly likely.

Note in Table 4.4 that the World GDP growth rate for the whole period, 2012–2100, is similar in Piketty's forecast and in ours; both round up to 2.3%. The significant difference in the previous indicator appears in the period of 2050–2100 (1.5% in Piketty's scenario versus 2.1% in ours). There are three reasons for this difference. The first one lies in the population forecast which is slightly different in our scenario due to the fact that we have used the most recent World Population Prospects (June 2013 version) of the United Nations instead of the one used by Piketty (April 2011 version). But this explains only a very small part of the difference since even if we had worked with the population forecast used by Piketty, the World GDP growth rate would have been 1.98% (not a significant difference with our value). The second reason is that our scenario does not distinguish between the first and the second half of the twenty-first century, because such a distinction seems, in our opinion, almost impossible to forecast. The third reason, which is closely related to the previous one, is the regional distribution of the product. Contrary to the scenario posed by Piketty, our scenario refuses the rapid convergence of the underdeveloped countries and maintains the relative importance of the wealthy countries in the global economy (see Table 4.3).

In particular, observe that in Piketty's scenario the developed world halves its participation, while Sub-Saharan Africa goes from 2.6% to 16.5%, Northern Africa from 1.4% to 3% and India from 5.7% to 11.9%. In our scenario, Western Europe and Japan reduce their participation but less drastically than with Piketty, North America actually increases its participation slightly. China and the other Asian countries, which with Piketty only maintain their participation, will increase it. Sub-Saharan Africa and Northern Africa mostly maintain their participation, while India increases it but much less than with Piketty. Eastern Europe and Russia will lose participation, as with Piketty. Latin-America decreases its participation in our scenario, while it increases it with Piketty.

Even though we do not have a real basis to forecast which countries will converge in the twenty-first century and which ones will not, most likely some will continue converging in the second half and some new comers will join. So, it seems that the most probable event is that the convergence phenomenon will help sustain a higher growth rate of the global economy for a long time to come. In particular China, with its enormous population, will take long time to converge. As social needs increase, the speed of convergence will go down, but it will continue for a very long time. In a similar case is India. There are just no reasons to forecast that the convergence will happen as fast as Piketty has argued. Thus, everything indicates that Pikketty's convergence is way too aggressive.

In summary, the dynamics of g in Piketty's model mainly depends on two events: 1) the end of the fast technological development which reduces the rate of economic growth of the developed countries, and 2) the end of poverty due to the rapid announced convergence. Both events seem to us highly unlikely. An alternative scenario was built in which g for the second half of the twenty-first century is 2.1% versus Piketty's 1.5%.

Chapter 5

Conclusion

Analyzing together the dynamics of r, s and g, we can build diverse stationary state scenarios for the second half of the twenty-first century. For g we use two values: Piketty's 1.5% and the 2.1% from the scenario that we propose. For s_n we use three values for each g. At $g = 1.5\%$ we use $s_n = 10\%$ from Piketty; $s_n = 7.96\%$ coming from a Solow model with s_b fixed at its 1990–2010 average value, Table 3.1; and $s_n = 6.40\%$ coming from Table 3.3 in which we allowed for s_b to go down accordingly with the experience in the developed countries. At $g = 2.1\%$ we use again the 10% from Piketty; 9.79% which corresponds to Solow model with fixed s_b, Table 3.1; and 8.07% which is the value obtained allowing s_b to go down, Table 3.3. For r before taxes we will take several values: the 4.3% from Piketty and the r that corresponds to each pair formed by the estimated β and the estimate of the gross elasticity of substitution between capital and labor: the 0.406 and 0.857 from Chirinko and Mallick (2014), and the 1.25 from Karabarbounis and Neiman (2014), see Table 2.6. Since there are three estimated β for each one of the two g's, and three σ^{gross} for each β, we will have a total of eighteen estimated r's. For the difference between the r before and after taxes we will take three values: 1) the zero tax, t_0, in Piketty's forecast, Table 2.8; 2) capital taxes of 30%, which is the assumption made by Piketty for the period 1950 to 2012, see the comment below; and 3) capital taxes at 20%. Table 5.1 shows the diverse scenarios.

What is the initial reference? r before taxes for the period 1990–2012 is 4.3%, Supplemental Table S6.2 (Excel version) of Piketty (2014). And the r after taxes for the same period would be 3.01% (4.3% × 0.7); see Piketty (2014) Supplemental Table S10.3. where he uses a tax rate of 0.7 for the period of 1950 to 2012. Piketty also deducts 0.5% due to public firms profits in the period of 1950–2012 which we are not considering in order to have the same basis of comparison going forward. β for 2010 is 440%, Piketty (2014) Supplemental Table S12.4.a. Therefore, using the previous data the reference is: α before taxes of 18.92% (or 440 × 0.043), and α after taxes of 13.24% (or 440 × 0.0301). Lets us now discuss. What does Table 5.1 tell us?

In scenarios 1.1 to 6.3 (with R.C denoting the corresponding row and column from Table 5.1) r is fixed at 4.3%, Piketty's assumption. Scenarios 1.4 to 6.12 use an estimated r, which takes into account the sensitivity of r in relationship to the value taken by β according to diverse values of σ^{gross} (denoted simply as σ hereafter): 0.406, 0.857 and 1.25.

Table 5.1: Alternative scenarios for α

		$g = 1.5\%$														
		$r = 4.3\%$				$\sigma^{gross} = 0.406$				$\sigma^{gross} = 0.857$				$\sigma^{gross} = 1.25$		
		C1	C2	C3		C4	C5	C6		C7	C8	C9		C10	C11	C12
	β (%)	t_0	t_{30}	t_{20}	r_{est}	t_0	t_{30}	t_{20}	r_{est}	t_0	t_{30}	t_{20}	r_{est}	t_0	t_{30}	t_{20}
R1	667 ($s_n = 10\%$)	28.67	20.06	22.93	-1.5	0.00	0.00	0.00	1.55	10.35	7.24	8.28	2.42	16.11	11.28	12.89
R2	531 ($s_n = 7.96\%$)	22.82	15.98	18.26	1.38	7.34	5.14	5.87	2.92	15.49	10.84	12.39	3.35	17.79	12.46	14.24
R3	427 ($s_n = 6.40\%$)	18.35	12.85	14.68	4.83	20.61	14.43	16.49	4.55	19.42	13.59	15.54	4.47	19.08	13.36	15.27

| | | $g = 2.1\%$ | | | | | | | | | | | | | | |
| | | $r = 4.3\%$ | | | | $\sigma^{gross} = 0.406$ | | | | $\sigma^{gross} = 0.857$ | | | | $\sigma^{gross} = 1.25$ | | |
	β (%)	t_0	t_{30}	t_{20}	r_{est}	t_0	t_{30}	t_{20}	r_{est}	t_0	t_{30}	t_{20}	r_{est}	t_0	t_{30}	t_{20}
R4	476 ($s_n = 10\%$)	20.48	14.33	16.38	3.00	14.30	10.01	11.44	3.69	17.55	12.29	14.04	3.88	18.47	12.93	14.78
R5	466 ($s_n = 9.79\%$)	20.04	14.03	16.03	3.34	15.58	10.91	12.47	3.85	17.93	12.55	14.35	3.99	18.60	13.02	14.88
R6	384 ($s_n = 8.07\%$)	16.53	11.57	13.22	6.77	26.01	18.21	20.81	5.47	21.02	14.72	16.82	5.10	19.61	13.73	15.69

Note: column C1 is equal to $0.043 \times \beta$, C2 is equal to $(0.043 \times 0.7)\beta$, and C3 is $(0.043 \times 0.8)\beta$. In columns C4 to C12 we use the same calculations as in Table 2.6

The first two lessons of Table 5.1 are that with the law of decreasing returns operating, according to empirical evidence on σ, all the increases in s_n, as well as the falls in g, produce the opposite results to the ones argued by Piketty. In Piketty's world with both s_n and r relatively stable, if s_n goes up or g goes down, β goes up and α also goes up. In the world of decreasing returns if s_n goes up or g goes down, β goes up but α goes down. This is due to powerful decreasing returns so that the increases in β are related to higher proportional reductions in r. Notice that in Table 5.1: 1) when g falls from 2.1% to 1.5%, in Piketty's world, columns C1 to C3, both β and α go up, while in the decreasing returns world, columns C4 to C12, β goes up but α goes down. 2) In Piketty's world, columns C1 to C3, when s_n goes up, β and α also go up; while in the world of decreasing returns, columns C4 to C12, when s_n goes up, β goes up but α goes down.

If we look only at Piketty's world: scenario 1.1 Piketty's forecast, β goes up from 440% in 2010 to 667% in 2100, an increase of 51.6% and α after taxes also goes up from 13.24% in 2010 to 28.7% in 2100, an increase of 116.7%. Scenarios 1.2 and 1.3 show the sensitivity of α to the assumption made on taxes. 1.2 shows that the rise in α in Piketty's scenario can be decomposed in two effects: 1) An increase of 51.6% $\left(\frac{16.74}{11.04} = 1.516\right)$ which, with r fixed, is explained by the rise in β; and 2) An increase of 143% explained by the assumption of zero taxes.

Scenarios 2.1 and 3.1, 5.1 and 6.1 show the β sensitivity to s_n. With $s_n = 6.40\%$ β actually goes down slightly.

If we look only at the world of decreasing returns. The first observation, as we mentioned already is that: at any value of σ less than the equilibrium value of 1.6—the empirical relevant values—decreasing returns imply that when β goes up, α goes down. The second observation is that when β goes down we face increasing returns. Nothing new, scarcity brings value. Note in Table 5.1 that in rows R3 and R6—columns C4 to C12—the fall in β produces increasing returns, therefore α goes up and it is higher than the respective references. The third observation is that the world of decreasing returns manifests that $s_n = 10\%$ at $g = 1.5\%$, is probably too high; notice first that in all cases the estimated r's in row R1 are too low; second α is zero at $\sigma = 0.406$, very low at $\sigma = 0.857$ and still low at $\sigma = 1.25$. Using Solow's model (Table 3.1), the estimated r's increase but they are still low compared to historical standards, remember that the average on 1990–2010 was 4.3%, the reason is the increase in β to 531% versus the historical 2010 β of 440%. Using a model that takes into account the fall in s_b related to the lower g (Table 3.3), β only falls slightly compared to 2010, and r is also slightly higher, in the range of 4.47% to 4.55%. Because β falls it triggers increasing returns and α goes up but very moderately, in the range 19.08–19.42, versus the initial 18.92. The fourth observation is that when σ goes up α may go up or down depending on whether β has increased or decreased. If $\beta_2/\beta_1 > 1$, then as σ goes up α goes up. If $\beta_2/\beta_1 < 1$, then as σ goes up α goes down. But remember that both $\sigma = 0.857$ and $\sigma = 1.25$ already include the effect of σ going up in the long run. The fifth observation is that there is an interaction between all of the variables, for example compare the scenario 2.10 with 5.10; α is higher in 5.10, despite the fact that β is lower. The reason is that r is significantly higher in 5.10 due to the lower β as a consequence of the decreasing returns. Also note that β is lower in 5.10 despite the fact that s_n is higher; this is consequence of the higher g.

For what we have been arguing Piketty's forecast has serious difficulties. His main problem is that letting r and s_n relatively rigid, he does not take into account the technological constraints of the production function and its consequences in a world where economic agents optimize. The outcome is that Piketty's results are neither theoretically or empirically satisfactory. Markets do work, economic agents optimize and the law of decreasing returns is powerful as the empirical evidence of an $\sigma < 1.25$ shows. Not only r goes down proportionally more to the β increases, but also s_b and s_n are both a positive function of g.

It is practically impossible to forecast what will happen in the twenty-first century. As we have been showing, the forecasted results are extremely sensitive to the assumptions made. Moreover, in the real world there may always be speculative waves and price effects. However, long-run forecasts cannot be based in such medium-term distortions that cannot be forecasted. We would like to insist that the most likely long-term forecast is shown in rows R3 and R6, because in them markets are fully operational. These two rows take into account both the law of decreasing returns and the fact that both s_b and s_n are a positive function of g. In addition, as to the value of σ, as we argued previously, one should probably be inclined to the range of 0.857–1.25, because these values take into account long-term global effects as the markets change their modes of production. Therefore, it seems that if one is to believe that g will be as low as Piketty's forecast (1.5%), then α before taxes will most likely be in the range between 19.08 and 19.42; very close to its initial value of 18.92. Whereas, if one believes that g will be higher (2.1%), then α before taxes will be in the range between 19.61 and 21.02. In the other hand, α after taxes is of course highly sensitive to the tax policy. However, as long as the tax policy remains the same, the results after taxes and before taxes are identical. In Table 5.1, with capital taxes at 30%, the level used for building the initial α reference, whenever α before taxes is higher or lower than the initial reference before taxes, α after taxes is also higher or lower than the initial reference after taxes. At $g = 1.5\%$, α after taxes, using the same row and columns than before, will be in a range between 13.36 and 13.59, again very close to its initial reference value of 13.24. At $g = 2.1\%$, α after taxes will be in the range of 13.73 to 14.72.

The income distribution between the factors of production, as we always knew, is mostly related to the tax policy. With capital taxes of 20% at $g = 1.5\%$ the range for α after taxes will be 15.27 to 15.54 and at $g = 2.1\%$ the range will be 15.69 to 16.82. Both ranges are not only higher than the initial reference of 13.74, but also, obviously, higher than the ranges at capital taxes at 30%, which tell us the importance of the tax policy.

There is not an invisible hand that guarantees that the income distribution amongst the factors of production will be inherently stable. But neither is there an invisible hand that will drive capitalism necessarily towards income concentration in favor of the capitalists. Markets do work and it is difficult to envision that only due to economic forces the income distribution will worsen significantly; and in any case, if this were to happen, it would be due to capital scarcity and not due to capital abundance as Piketty has suggested.

There are powerful medium-term forces that can seriously distort the income distribution amongst the factors of production, like speculative housing waves and other price effects; there are all sort of institutional factors that may in real life worsen the income distribution; and there may also be powerful political forces pushing for policies that may deteriorate the income distribution (see Acemoglu and Robinson, 2015). Therefore, governments and the society have to be always alert as to the dynamics of the income distribution in each particular case. But, in the long run the income distribution amongst the factors of production will not, only due to economic forces, tend towards the pronounced concentration in favor of capital that Piketty has argued.

Epilogue

In this epilogue we briefly make some very general remarks on four topics related to Pikety's proposal of the general dynamics of capitalism. The first topic is related to the discussion of whether the income distribution is still a good measure of the actual income "enjoyment" by the participants in the economy. The second one has to do with discussing the meaning of income distribution. The third topic is related to the personal income distribution in the World Top Incomes Database (WTID). The fourth one is about the dynamics of capitalism.

E.1 Income enjoyment

Piketty's discussion mainly relates to income distribution and it does not include in a systematic way the analysis of the consequences of government expenditures. The limitations of not focusing in transfer payments have been pointed out by Auerbach and Hassett (2015). This point is particularly crucial in the developed world in which governments control about 40% of the national income, when they only controlled around 10% in the beginning of the twenty-first century. What Piketty has called the patrimonial class is politically and economically significantly better at the beginning of the twenty-first century in relationship to the same period in the twentieth century. Few calculations show that this is the case, but to take this point seriously probably deserves another book of the same size of Piketty's. The first two columns in Table E.1 show the share of income of the richest decile in the United States, the United Kingdom and France in 1900 and 2010; columns 3 and 4 show the tax revenues of the government on the same dates; and column five shows the percentage dedicated to social spending. Table E.2 shows a very rough calculation on the assumptions that: 1) in 1900 social spending was minimal and total government expenditures equally affects the richest 10% and the remaining 90%; 2) in 2010 it is assumed that all social spending goes to the less rich 90% and that the non-social spending equally affects the richest 10% and the remaining 90%. The results are the outcome of a very rough calculation but they are striking. In the United States, despite the fact that the 10% has 47.9% of national income in 2010, versus 40.5% in 1900, once government expenditures are introduced, the 10% enjoys only 34% in 2010 versus 38% in 1900. In the U.K., the 10% has 41.6% of the income in 2010 versus 47.1% in 1900; and the 10% enjoys only 26% of the income in 2010 versus 44% in 1900. In France the 10% has 33% of the income in 2010 versus 45.5% in 1900; and the 10% enjoys only 18% in 2010 versus 43% in 1900. This rough calculation clearly shows the point that we wanted to illustrate. Democracy, in the developed economies, has implied that the less rich 90% of the population have gained

Table E.1: Income, tax revenues and social spending

Country	Income share richest 10% 1900	Income share richest 10% 2010	Tax revenues 1900	Tax revenues 2010	Social spending as % of public spending 2000–2010
U.S.	40.5	47.9	7	31	63.27
U.K.	47.1	41.6	8	40	69.39
France	45.5	33.0	8	49	67.25

Source: Supplementary Tables S9.4, S13.1 and S13.2 of Piketty (2014), available online at `http://piketty.pse.ens.fr/en/capital21c2`.

Table E.2: A very rough calculation. Income enjoyment: the richest 10% vs. the remaining 90%

Country	1900 10%	1900 90%	2010 10%	2010 90%
U.S.	38	62	34	62
U.K.	44	56	26	74
France	43	57	18	82

Source: Calculation based in Table E.1. It is very rough and only intends to give a general idea

significant command on the enjoyment of national income.

In the developing world the story is very different because the government's size is smaller. Therefore social expenditures in these countries are less significant, while for example the high human-development countries had 17.5 % of GDP in public spending on health and education, the medium to low human-development countries only spent around half of that, 8.6% of GDP (data from United Nations Human Development Report 2014).

The economic strength of the 90% in developed countries has had much to do with the growth in the global economy; it has definitely increased the global market size. In fact the dynamic preferences of a large middle class have been a necessary guidance for the rapid technological development in the developed western countries.

E.2 What do we mean by income distribution?

When we talk about income distribution we can do it at least at three different levels: countries, factors of production and individuals. If we look at the global income distribution between individuals it is highly unequal. Just to give a reference, today the world is more unequal than Brazil. And to explain this extreme global inequality, Milanovic (2013) has shown that the inequality between countries is much more decisive than the inequality among individuals within a country. Today the country to which a given individual belongs explains more than 50% of his future per-capita income. Therefore the critical issue in the dynamics of capitalism does not seem to be the conflict between economic classes, but the conflict between nations.

E.3 The personal income distribution in the WTID database

Analyzing the WTID database, one can see that there is not the announced long-run necessary tendency towards the concentration of income in favour of the richest 10%. Table E.3 shows the average income share of the richest 10% for two periods for each country, the methodology has been to divide the total years by half, starting in the first year that data is available after 1900 and ending in the last year found for each country. Missing years are in all cases filled with the data from the previous year available. Of the twelve countries presented only two concentrate the income in favor of the richest 10%: Australia and Japan.

Table E.3: Income share of the richest 10%

Country	Years first period	Years second period
	1941–1975	1976–2010
Australia	29.09	37.35
Canada	37.95	37.35
	1903–1957	1958–2010
Denmark	37.70	27.50
	1905–1957	1958–2009
France	40.11	33.14
	1900–1949	1950–1998
Germany	37.37	32.23
	1947–1978	1979–2010
Japan	30.60	35.41
	1914–1963	1964–2012
Netherlands	41.71	29.58
	1906–1958	1959–2011
Norway	34.72	28.33
	1903–1957	1958–2012
Sweden	38.15	26.43
	1933-1971	1972-2009
Switzerland	31.10	30.88
	1918–1964	1965–2011
U.K.	35.91	34.37
	1917–1964	1965–2012
U.S.	38.06	37.85

Source: WTID database, September 2014, available online at
http://topincomes.parisschoolofeconomics.eu.

E.4 The dynamics of capitalism

The discussion as to whether Piketty is right or wrong has relevance. After all, we are discussing the central dynamics of capitalism and the required economic policies. For Piketty, the dynamics is given by fundamental economic laws that necessarily concentrate income in favor of the capitalists, laws that have to be opposed by the institutions. Thus, there is in Piketty an inherent economic conflict between the most privileged and the rest of the population. Moreover, with his convergence mechanism he gets rid of the unequal income distribution between countries. As we have been discussing he is wrong. The main conflict to be resolved, as far as income distribution is concerned, is between nations, not between classes. The world has a lot to gain if the developed countries seriously commit themselves to the growth of the developing ones.

In the developed countries there is a clear triumph of the masses as to the size of the economic resources that they enjoy. And the rapid development of the middle class in these countries has been a motor engine for the growth of the whole world. The growing middles class has enlarged the market to unprecedented levels; and the dynamic process of their changing preferences has lead to technological change in the west—this was the crucial difference with Russia for example. It must be remarked, that the growing middle class in the west not only explains the rapid development of this region, but it has also been the key in the success of the Asian miracle whose economic model is based upon exports to the middle class in the west. One of the key problems in the developing economies is that they do not have the required middle class size.

Piketty emphasizes a groundless economic dynamics—one which necessarily implies class conflict—and he undermines the two crucial factors that have characterized global capitalism: the rapid growth of the middle class in developed countries and the lasting highly unequal distribution between countries.

Bibliography

Daron Acemoglu and James A. Robinson. The Rise and Decline of General Laws of Capitalism. *Journal of Economic Perspectives*, 29(1):3–28, 2015. URL http://www.aeaweb.org/articles.php?doi=10.1257/jep.29.1.3.

Alan J. Auerbach and Kevin Hassett. Capital Taxation in the Twenty-First Century. *American Economic Review*, 105(5):48–53, 2015. URL http://dx.doi.org/10.1257/aer.p20151060.

Odran Bonnet, Pierre-Henri Bono, Guillaume Chapelle, and Étienne Wasmer. Does housing capital contribute to inequality? A comment on Thomas Piketty's Capital in the 21st Century. Sciences Po Economics Discussion Papers 2014-07, Sciences Po Departement of Economics, July 2014. URL http://spire.sciencespo.fr/hdl:/2441/30nstiku669glbr6616n7mc2oq/.

Robert S. Chirinko and Debdulal Mallick. The Substitution Elasticity, Factor Shares, Long-Run Growth, and the Low-Frequency Panel Model. CESifo Working Paper Series 4895, CESifo Group Munich, October 2014. URL http://papers.ssrn.com/sol3/papers.cfm?abstract_id=2479816.

Charles I. Jones. The Shape of Production Functions and the Direction of Technical Change. *The Quarterly Journal of Economics*, 120(2):517–549, 2005. URL http://qje.oxfordjournals.org/content/120/2/517.abstract.

Loukas Karabarbounis and Brent Neiman. The Global Decline of the Labor Share. *The Quarterly Journal of Economics*, 129(1):61–103, 2014. URL http://qje.oxfordjournals.org/content/129/1/61.abstract.

Per Krusell and Antony A. Smith. Is Piketty's "Second law of Capitalism" Fundamental?, May 2015. URL http://aida.wss.yale.edu/smith/piketty1.pdf. (*to be published*).

Debdulal Mallick. The Role of the Elasticity of Substitution in Economic Growth: A Cross-Country Test of the de La Grandville Hypothesis. Economics Series 4, Deakin University, Faculty of Business and Law, School of Accounting, Economics and Finance, May 2007. URL http://www.deakin.edu.au/buslaw/aef/workingpapers/papers/2007_04eco.pdf.

Debdulal Mallick. The role of the elasticity of substitution in economic growth: A cross-country investigation. *Labour Economics*, 19(5):682–694, 2012. URL http://www.sciencedirect.com/science/article/pii/S0927537112000310.

Branko Milanovic. Global Income Inequality in Numbers: in History and Now. *Global Policy*, 4(2):198–208, 2013. ISSN 1758-5899. URL http://dx.doi.org/10.1111/1758-5899.12032.

Ezra Oberfield and Devesh Raval. Micro Data and Macro Technology. NBER Working Papers 20452, National Bureau of Economic Research, September 2014. URL http://www.nber.org/papers/w20452.

Thomas Piketty. *Capital in the Twenty-First century*. Harvard University Press, April 2014.

Thomas Piketty. About Capital in the Twenty-First Century. *American Economic Review*, 105(5):48–53, 2015. URL http://dx.doi.org/10.1257/aer.p20151060.

Thomas Piketty and Gabriel Zucman. Capital is Back: Wealth-Income Ratios in Rich Countries 1700–2010. *The Quarterly Journal of Economics*, 129(3):1255–1310, 2014. URL http://qje.oxfordjournals.org/content/129/3/1255.abstract.

Matthew Rognlie. A note on Piketty and diminishing returns to capital, June 2014. URL http://www.mit.edu/~mrognlie/piketty_diminishing_returns.pdf.

Matthew Rognlie. Deciphering the fall and rise in the net capital share, March 2015. URL http://www.brookings.edu/about/projects/bpea/papers/2015/land-prices-evolution-capitals-share.

Robert M. Solow. Thomas Piketty Is Right: Everything you need to know about 'Capital in the Twenty-First Century', April 2014. URL http://www.newrepublic.com/article/117429/.

David N. Weil. Capital and Wealth in the Twenty-First Century. *American Economic Review*, 105(5):34–37, May 2015. URL http://dx.doi.org/10.1257/aer.p20151057.

www.ingramcontent.com/pod-product-compliance
Lightning Source LLC
Chambersburg PA
CBHW081615170526
45166CB00009B/2971